Warm Smiles from Cold Mountains

Warm Smiles from Cold Mountains

Dharma Talks on
Zen Meditation

REB ANDERSON
Foreword by Susan Moon

RODMELL PRESS
Berkeley, California
1999

Permissions and appreciations appear on page 169.

Printed in the United States of America
04 03 02 01 00 99 1 2 3 4 5 6 7 8 9
ISBN 0-9627138-7-2
Library of Congress Catalog Card Number: 98-67482

Editors
Susan Moon
Donald Moyer

Copy Editor
Katherine L. Kaiser

Production Editor
Linda Cogozzo

Cover and Text Design and Composition
Jeanne M. Hendrickson
Hendrickson Design

Lithography
McNaughton & Gunn, Inc.

Text set in Centaur and Futura

Homage to our great original teacher, Shakyamuni Buddha.

Homage to the whole succession of disciples in the way.

Homage to the radical liberator in China, Bodhidharma.

Homage to our lofty ancestor of eternal peace, Eihei Dogen.

Homage to our compassionate founder, Shogaku Shunryu.

Contents

Acknowledgments

xiii

Foreword by Susan Moon

xv

PART ONE: PRACTICING DEEPLY

Great Wisdom Beyond Wisdom Heart Sutra

3

ONE

The Acupuncture Needle of Zazen

5

TWO

A Ceremony for the Encouragement of Zazen

I I

THREE

A Field Far Beyond Form and Emptiness

21

FOUR

Sitting in the Heart of Suffering

29

FIVE

The Five *Skandhas*

35

SIX

Just Sitting

47

PART TWO: EMBRACING ALL BEINGS

The Sixteen Great Bodhisattva Precepts
59

SEVEN

Speaking the Unspoken
61

EIGHT

Life Is Not Killed
73

NINE

The Home Altar
85

TEN

Just This Person
89

ELEVEN

Longing for Oneness
95

TWELVE

Cooking in the Cauldron of All Beings
99

PART THREE: TIME AND SEASON

Song of the Jewel Mirror Samadhi
107

THIRTEEN

Warm Smiles from Cold Mountains
111

FOURTEEN

Suchness
117

FIFTEEN

Listen to the Body
123

SIXTEEN

The Path of Peace Has No Sign
129

SEVENTEEN

Father's Day
139

EIGHTEEN

The End of Suffering: A Christmas Koan
151

APPENDIX

Notes
165

Appreciations
169

Acknowledgments

Innumerable beings contributed directly and indirectly to this little book. I thank them all and, in particular, I want to name a few of them. Throughout the years, many inspiring and patient students and teachers of Zen have invited me to speak about something that is vital to me: the practice of Zen meditation. Those who wanted to make these talks available to a wider audience encouraged me to put them in written form and gather them into a book. Meiya Wender provided the initial impetus for this project, did much of the editing, and generally expedited the production of the first edition. Susan Moon was the principal editor of the first edition, selecting, editing, and arranging the entire manuscript. The first edition was designed by Rosalie Curtis.

For the second edition, I added Chapter Two, "A Ceremony for the Encouragement of Zazan." Donald Moyer edited this edition, suggesting the current order of chapters and the division of the manuscript into three sections. Setsuan Godwin and Charlie Pokorny made many editorial improvements throughout the manuscript. Diana Gerard provided invaluable overall assistance, from footnoting various sources to acquiring permission for reprinting quotations. Katherine L. Kaiser copyedited the second edition of this book.

Many other people have transcribed and edited these talks throughout the years. I would especially like to thank the people who helped me to edit the earlier versions of these talks that appeared in San Francisco Zen Center's publication *Wind Bell:* Shosan Austin, Peter Bailey, Rusa Chiu, Sonja Gardenswartz, Jane Hirshfield, Michael Katz, Myo Lahey, Jeffrey Schneider, Furyu Schroeder, Laurie Senauke, Meiya Wender, and Michael Wenger. Leslie Boies edited "Father's Day," and Susan Moon edited "The Acupuncture Needle of Zazen" and "Life Is Not Killed," all of which originally appeared in *Turning Wheel: Journal of the Buddhist Peace Fellowship.*

Lastly, I would like to thank my daughter Thea Anderson, for teaching me to be a father by insisting on being herself, and Rusa Chiu, for her immeasurable and undefinable contribution.

I bow deeply to you all.

Reb Anderson
Green Dragon Temple
Green Gulch Farm
Muir Beach, California
October 1998

Foreword

The book in your hand, a sheaf of white leaves with black markings on them, started out as a voice—the voice of Reb Anderson—speaking in a Zen temple. The chapters were originally dharma talks, given at Tassajara Zen Mountain Center, Green Gulch Farm, or The City Center, some of my favorite places in the world. I would like to set the stage for you, tell you a little of what you cannot know from the words on the page: the smells, the sounds, the bodily experience.

I had the good fortune to be a monk at Tassajara a couple of winters ago, and to hear some of these talks when they were first given, down in that valley, deep in the mountains. During the winter practice period, lectures are scheduled for midmorning. The zendo is cold. The sun is up, but its light doesn't yet reach down the valley to warm the zendo roof. The morning dew is still dripping off the eaves.

The stream outside the zendo sings a constant song, like breath, swelling or softening according to the rains. The caw of blue jays punctuates Reb's words. Well-trimmed kerosene lanterns around the room burn steadily, reflecting off polished wood. And the people around the room, sitting on raised platforms in our black robes, we are lanterns, too, burning our calories, breathing our way from moment to moment, a family of us, become intimate through the long months of sitting together in these quiet mountains, this protected space.

Even inside the zendo, you can smell the freshness of the mountain air. And, of course, you smell incense. If the lecture lasts a long time, longer than the schedule says, then the kitchen crew has to leave before it's over to fix our lunch. So while they cook for us, we listen, for them. The jays outside grow noisier, greeting the sun as it reaches down into the valley.

Some of the talks were given at Green Gulch Farm. Green Gulch is another valley, a valley by the sea, where the air is moist and soft. Sometimes, in the zendo, you can hear the ocean waves. You can hear frogs peeping in the nearby pond, and sometimes the distant swoosh of a car passing up on Route One. At both Tassajara and Green Gulch, the listeners are nestled together in a valley, in a bowl, in the palm of Buddha's hand. The words of the lecture, along with the frogs, along with the rattle of the garbage truck, are filling a silver bowl with snow, pouring milk into milk.

Reb offers himself up in his talks, like the stream. There is something devotional about the way he speaks, a willingness to make contact in each moment. He sits upright. His voice is gentle, but remarkably intense for its softness. Sometimes he speaks slowly, sometimes in a flood of words, and always as if there is all the time in the world. And there is. He pauses, he looks out at us, he asks from time to time, "Are you with me?" "Are you hungry?" "Shall we sing a song?"

The words blend, seamlessly, with the jays, so that the jays, too, are saying, "Listen to this body. Life is not killed."

He is demanding. He asks us to stretch our understanding to the limit. "Approaching colors is not just the colors being the colors, but you approaching them. This is misery." What does he mean? Black cushions, gleaming brown wood reflecting lantern light, the green of someone's sock, peeking out from under her robes. Or, through the open door, a pink explosion of crab apple. "But if we do not approach these phenomena, if there is no seam between them and us, then these very same *skandhas*, these very same colors and sounds, are bliss."

Because we're all in the soup together, Reb brings in all of our stories. Some of the stories are about himself: about a dog he had as a kid, about what it feels like to be a father, about cleaning up his desk. He mixes the old Zen teaching stories of the ancestors with stories of students and friends. We hear about Good Servant, who sees his reflection in a river and is enlightened. We hear of an anxious monk at Tassajara who comforted herself by chopping turnips. We hear the story of Dogen walking around a pillar before his death, and the story of a student who was worried about her loud swallowing during zazen. All these stories are equally worthy.

Now the talks have become chapters in a book, and more people can read them. But the words still have the immediacy of Reb's voice. We can still feel his wholeheartedness, his commitment to sharing himself with his listeners and now with his readers. He does not hold back. And he calls forth our deep response, as well. Again and again, he reminds us that we're intimately connected and already Buddha. "Each of you—not separately, but in the cauldron with all beings, cooking and being cooked—is realizing awakening."

Susan Moon
Berkeley, California
August 1994

PART ONE

✸

PRACTICING DEEPLY

Great Wisdom Beyond Wisdom
Heart Sutra

Avalokiteshvara Bodhisattva, when deeply practicing *prajna paramita*, clearly saw that all five aggregates are empty, and thus relieved all suffering.

"O Shariputra, form does not differ from emptiness, emptiness does not differ from form: form itself is emptiness; emptiness itself is form. The same is true of feelings, perceptions, formations, and consciousness.

"O Shariputra, all dharmas are marked with emptiness: they do not appear or disappear, are not tainted or pure, and do not increase or decrease. Therefore, in emptiness, no form, no feelings, no perceptions, no formations, no consciousness; no eyes, no ears, no nose, no tongue, no body, no mind, no color, no sound, no smell, no taste, no touch, no object of mind; no realm of eyes, until no realm of mind-consciousness; no ignorance and also no extinction of it, until no old age and death, and also no extinction of it; no suffering, no origination, no stopping, no path, no cognition, also no attainment.

"With nothing to attain, a bodhisattva depends on *prajna paramita* and the mind is no hindrance. Without any hindrance, no fears exist. Far apart from every perverted view, one dwells in nirvana. In the three worlds, all buddhas depend on *prajna paramita* and attain unsurpassed complete and perfect enlightenment.

"Therefore, know the *prajna paramita* mantra is the great transcendent mantra, is the great bright mantra, is the utmost mantra, is the supreme mantra, which is able to relieve all suffering and which is true, not false.

"So proclaim the *prajna paramita* mantra, proclaim the mantra that says *Gate, gate, paragate, parasamgate! Bodhi! Svaha!*"

ONE

✸

The Acupuncture Needle of Zazen

What I want to talk about is zazen. Zazen is sitting upright in the present moment, right here, in the midst of Buddha's mind. There is a text about zazen by the great teacher Dogen Zenji, *Zazen Shin*. There are two ways of understanding this title. *Zazen* means—well, no one knows what it means—zazen is zazen. *Shin* means "needle," particularly the bamboo needles that were used in the old days for acupuncture. The first way to understand this title is that zazen is a needle that we stick into our lives; it's the needle with which we care for life. If we put this zazen needle in the right place, it will tenderize our lives. We will become sensitive to the totality of our lives, tender to all beings, so responsive that we realize how deeply connected we all are. This tenderness transforms ourselves and others. This is what happens when we understand zazen as an acupuncture treatment for our lives. The other way to understand *zazen shin* is as a medicine for zazen itself. It's a needle to treat our attempts to practice zazen. It's a medicine to treat our misunderstanding of the practice of zazen.

When we first begin, most of us practice zazen just as we do other things. We practice zazen to get something out of it, to improve some situation. We practice zazen as though there were something we could do by

5

ourselves. We understand the self as something that can do things—do Buddhist practice, do zazen—and this misunderstanding is deeply ingrained in us. This is normal; we all do this.

Dogen Zenji wrote, "When you first approach the way, you remove yourself from its neighborhood." When you first approach Buddhist practice, you go away from it just by the very fact that you are approaching it, rather than realizing it on the spot. We can't help this. We're looking to improve things. It's the way we see everything; it's unavoidable. Once we start practicing, we need treatment, we need a little medicine for our misunderstanding of what practice is. So may I insert a needle into your zazen practice?

First of all, zazen is a practice of living with all sentient beings. Zazen cannot be practiced one-sidedly. I cannot do zazen apart from you. You cannot do zazen apart from all of us. Zazen is realized in concert with all sentient beings. Good cannot be done by any one person. All good things are done together with all sentient beings.

Zazen is just like our lives and our lives are like riding in a boat. You can't ride in a boat by yourself. As Dogen Zenji says, you raise the sail, you sit up straight, you put your tongue on the roof of your mouth, you cross your legs, and you row with the oars. And although you row, the boat gives you a ride. Without the boat, no one could ride, but your riding makes the boat what it is. This realm of mutual creation with all sentient beings— where we make one another what we are—is the realm of zazen. Zazen is the way we care for our lives together.

We can care for our lives by ourselves, and that's the way we're accustomed to living. We have all done a pretty good job of it. You got this far because you did a good job of taking care of yourself by yourself. But this is not zazen. Now that you've taken care of yourself so well, you have a chance to enter the great mind of Buddha, to learn how to take care of yourself along with all sentient beings. This is "cultivating an empty field." Cultivating the empty field is the same as cultivating the sky. Do you know how to plow the clouds? This cloud farming is done with all sentient beings. It's also called zazen.

Someone once approached Suzuki Roshi and asked, "Why haven't you enlightened me yet?" Suzuki Roshi answered politely, "I'm making my best effort." He might have told the student to make more effort herself, but he didn't say that. He said "I'm making my best effort." Zazen is the way I care for my life with all beings. I can't do it by myself. Can you have faith in a way that you can't do by yourself? Most people can trust only a way that they do by themselves. But living a life that you can do by yourself is unadulterated misery. Completely trusting a way that you can't do by yourself, that you do with all sentient beings, is immediate liberation.

Some people say that Zen is hard to understand. It *is* hard to understand, but not because it's obscure. It's hard to understand because it's like the sky. Look at the blue sky. It's nice to look at, but it's hard to understand. It's so big and it goes on forever. How are you going to get

7

it? It's hard to understand all sentient beings, too, but it's not difficult to sit upright and be aware of them.

One day, a monk asked the great teacher Matsu, "What is Buddha's mind?"

Matsu said, "Mind itself is Buddha."

Later someone told Matsu, "I hear you said, 'Mind itself is Buddha.'"

"I say that to children, so they will stop crying."

"What do you say after they stop crying?"

"I say, 'No mind, no Buddha.'"

The practice of "no mind, no Buddha" is based on great faith. This is trusting what is actually happening. This is trusting "what." Put aside your doubts and trust it. Trust *what*. Don't trust *it*, a thing that you can think of. Trust what you *can't* think of. Trust the vastness of space. Trust every single living being. Trust cause and effect; vast, inconceivably complex, and wondrous cause and effect. This faith has unlimited possibilities. Think about not moving. Think about giving up all action. And remember, giving up all action does not mean stopping action. That would be another action. "Giving up" means giving up the attempt to do things by yourself, and embracing the way of doing things with everyone.

Trust Buddha's mind. Trusting Buddha's mind means trusting all sentient beings. This is fearless love. You can give it all up, and then you can love every single thing.

Dogen said, "Mind itself is Buddha. Practice is difficult; explanation is not difficult." People like a practice where you can explain how to do it. It feeds the deluded karmic mind. First you do this, and then you do that, and then you do this: people like this. But what is easy to explain is difficult to practice, because the explanations move us further away from the practice itself, and we need all kinds of antidotes to get us back on track. "No mind, no Buddha" is not difficult to practice, but it is difficult to explain. Sitting still is not difficult to practice, because it's just like the sky, but it's as difficult to understand as the sky.

Practicing goodness is like riding in a boat. When you make a bag lunch and give it to someone who is hungry or take a present to someone who is sick, if you think you are doing this by yourself, you're missing the point. You can't ride in a boat by yourself. You need the boat; the boat gives you a ride. If you make a lunch for someone, the food gives you a ride, the food makes it possible for you to make the lunch. All sentient beings give you the food. All sentient beings make the lunch through your hands and your eyes and your body. Without you, the lunch couldn't be made. Without them, the lunch couldn't be made. Now let me ask you: If the practice of all the buddhas and ancestors is being realized right now, who is it realized by?

If you answer "All beings," you're right. Yes—all beings! All beings are sharing the way at this moment. Never graspable, yet totally available. There is no other thing outside of this. My question is, do we trust it?

Looking at myself, the only thing I can find that holds me back from completely trusting the practice in which all sentient beings are now engaged is lack of courage: lack of courage to affirm all life, which is the same as the lack of courage to affirm death. Without being able to affirm death, I cannot affirm life. This is the courage that comes with insight, so I could say that what holds me back is a lack of insight.

When I'm with some sentient beings, I lack the courage to meet them. I'm afraid of what he or she may do, and what I may do in response. So I hold back, and by holding back, I don't affirm life. Holding back, I'm unable to care for the other person completely.

But I can make a vow, which, for me, is the same as practicing zazen. The vow will not be to meet each person completely by my own willpower. I will not make that vow. I will vow to trust that all sentient beings meet *in* my life, *as* my life. I will witness the arrival of all things as my life. That's my vow.

What will be your vow? Do you want to commit yourself to the way of Buddha, the way that all sentient beings practice together? Or do you wish to continue an ancient karmic pattern of living by your own willpower? Consider my question and tell me the answer. Again and again, tell me the answer, so I can understand the heart of your zazen, the heart of your love, the heart of your wisdom.

Green Dragon Temple
Green Gulch Farm
Muir Beach, California
July 4, 1993

TWO

A Ceremony for the Encouragement of Zazen

Zazen is the source of all the teachings and practices of the buddha way. Although the word *zazen* literally means "sitting concentration," it is not limited to concentration practice. All enlightened concentration practices emanate from and return to zazen. Here, one's mind is concentrated without relying on any contrivance and is not necessarily focused continuously on any particular object. There are concentration practices and if one is practicing thus, zazen is just being upright and unmoving in the midst of such a practice. If one is not practicing concentration, it is just sitting still in the middle of not practicing concentration. It is simply pure presence untouched by all human agency. Many people attempt to concentrate their minds and, according to their own definition, are unsuccessful. Practicing concentration in this way often leads to feeling frustrated and upset. Even if one is successful in achieving concentration by personal effort, the mind is still somewhat disturbed by such striving. In Buddha's meditation, there is no such striving. Giving up the desire to pacify the mind, pacifies the mind.

For this reason, if I give a beginner zazen instruction, although I usually suggest that she sit upright with

11

the spine straight, eyes open, and hands in the cosmic concentration mudra, I do not encourage bending the mind into concentrating on the posture or breathing, nor do I discourage it. If someone asks for instruction on how to concentrate on posture or breathing, I am happy to give detailed instruction on how to practice that way. Although concentration practices may be wonderfully beneficial and develop great mental skill, trying to concentrate on some object, such as the breath, may activate a gaining idea. Gaining ideas are antithetical to the whole project of Mahayana Buddhism, which is to be concerned for others' welfare rather than our own self-improvement. However, we may not realize this right from the start of our practice. As long as we are engaged in a self-improvement meditation, we continue to be trapped in ourselves. When we are free of self-improvement projects, we are free of ourselves.

Although it may be difficult to wholeheartedly concentrate on an object without getting caught in some self-serving gaining idea, it is also true that having a gaining idea may be an important step in one's cultivation and realization of a practice that is free of all such gaining ideas. Such practice may help one to forge a strong enough container to tolerate a nongaining approach to meditation. It frequently happens that if a practitioner pushes personal effort to the limit in a wholesome way, as in concentration practice, she can realize the futility of depending on personal power and then find another entrance into zazen.

The zazen I speak of is not concentration practice; neither is it not concentration practice. Zazen does not prefer success to failure. Zazen does not prefer enlighten-ment to delusion. If we are enlightened, we sit still in the middle of enlightenment with no preference for it. If we are deluded, we sit still in the middle of delusion with no aversion to it. This is Buddha's zazen.

The goal of zazen practice is the enlightenment and liberation of all living beings from suffering. That is the goal of zazen, but the goal is exactly the same as the practice. In realizing this goal, one becomes free of self-concern and personal gain; becoming free of self-concern and personal gain realizes the goal.

Although one might joyfully practice concentrat-ing on posture and breathing with no gaining idea, still, zazen is not limited to this form of practice. As our ancestor Dogen said, zazen is "totally culminated enlight-enment. Traps and snares can never reach it. Once its heart is grasped, you are like the dragon when he enters the water, like the tiger when she returns to the mountain." In other words, zazen survives every reduction. It cannot be reduced or trapped into mindfulness or mindlessness of the breath or of the posture. It cannot be captured by any activity of the human body or mind.

Zazen doesn't start when we start making effort, doesn't stop when we stop. However, when practicing zazen, there is complete mindfulness. and we may very well notice that we are breathing. It's not that our ordinary awareness isn't going on, it's just that the practice does not abide in, and cannot be defined by, the things we are aware of at the moment. As the great teacher Prajnatara said,

"This poor wayfarer, 'when breathing in, does not abide in the realms of body or mind, and when breathing out, does not get entangled in the various objects of experience.' I always recite this scripture." The breath of zazen is to be thoroughly intimate with, and liberated through, all realms of experience. This is the breathing of Buddha. Still, we may need to familiarize ourselves with, and become proficient in, the forms of concentration on breath and posture in order to develop enough confidence to selflessly practice the formless breathing of the "poor wayfarer."

Zazen is formless like vast space, yet it manifests forms in response to living beings, like the moon reflected in water. Because we may need forms to help us relate to the formless, when people first come to learn about zazen at a Zen center, they are given instructions in how to perform a formal ceremony of zazen. Beginners usually want to have some activity they can do, so we give them something to do. However, the zazen of our school is not something we can do. The ceremony is for tempering our tolerance for a formless practice that we cannot do. Strictly speaking, awakened Buddhist meditation is not an action done by a person: it is not another form of doing, not another form of karma. It is the function of enlightenment, the concerted activity of the entire universe.

Conventionally speaking, Zen students say, "Now I am going to the meditation hall to do zazen." However, the formal actions that you or I perform in assuming the traditional bodily posture of sitting meditation are not actually the zazen of the buddha ancestors. Their zazen has nothing to do with sitting or lying down. These ritual forms that we humans practice are a ceremony by which we express and celebrate our devotion to the actual reality of zazen.

The ceremonial forms are opportunities for people to embrace, and be embraced by, the inconceivable totality of zazen. They are dharma gateways for the body and mind to manifest the truth of zazen. The forms are ways for zazen to come into the body and accord with the mind.

When people are sitting during the ceremony of zazen, I sometimes walk around the room, adjusting their posture. This adjustment is intended as a silent comment on their posture. Although I am inspired by the beauty of people's effort in sitting upright and still, nevertheless I may have some suggestions that encourage more whole-hearted devotion to the ceremony of zazen.

Our physical posture reflects our participation in the ceremony, and our participation in the entire universe. Giving our posture entirely to the ceremony, we give our-selves entirely to the universe. Total devotion to one is total devotion to the other. Resistance to one is resistance to the other. On the one hand, if our spines are curved or hunched over, then our chests are caved in, our lungs are constricted, and our hearts are withdrawn. On the other hand, if our spines come deeper into our torsos so that we are sitting more upright, then we have more room for breathing and our hearts come forward. We feel more alive and, feeling more alive, we are more open and vulnerable to suffering, and enter more deeply into the joyful and vital realm where the wheel of dharma is turned.

When a person fully accepts her suffering by assuming this upright posture, she is released. Working with her posture in this way encourages her to fully experience what it means to have a body, to fully enter her own physical presence.

However, when people mistake the ceremony for zazen itself, they may develop a sense that there is a right way and a wrong way to practice zazen. Thus they may be uncomfortable entering a meditation hall because they don't want to do the wrong thing. For such people, the trap of thinking in terms of right and wrong can be undermining and distracting, so I might refer them to a less ceremonial form of meditation. This way, they can relax into sitting and walking meditation without getting caught up in worrying about concepts of right and wrong. Perhaps after bodies and minds are calm and stabilized by practicing a less ceremonial form of meditation, they might be able to return to formal Zen practice and deal fruitfully with any complications arising from issues of right and wrong.

For other people, the ceremonial forms provide a structure or refuge in which they can tolerate the formless, objectless practice of zazen. The ritual forms are a vessel in which they may enter into the inconceivable activity of enlightenment.

The meaning of zazen is not limited to the ceremony, but manifests in response to our devotion to the ceremony. As the "Song of the Jewel Mirror Samadhi" says, "The meaning is not in the words. Yet it responds to the arrival of energy." It manifests in response to the arrival of our energetic effort and devotion.

One of the fundamental texts of our school is the great teacher Dogen's *Ceremony for the Universal Encouragement of Zazen (Fukanzazengi)*. The Chinese word for *ceremony* in the title of this work is composed of two characters. The first character means "person," and the second means "justice, righteousness, or meaning." The ceremony provides an opportunity for the person to be united with the meaning of zazen. Zazen is the selfless practice that comes to meet our sincere devotion to the ceremony of zazen. The instructions are basically established procedures for a formal ceremony that we may perform in a meditation hall or at home. But zazen cannot be reduced to that ceremony. Zazen is happening all the time and everywhere; we do the ceremony within particular limits of time and space to celebrate the limitless, all-pervasive reality of zazen. This ceremony is the central religious act of the Zen school. In a Zen monastery, we may practice this ceremony all day long, but it is still just a ceremony, not the totality of zazen itself. Performing the ceremony heals any gap between our lives and the true zazen practice of Buddha.

In this ceremony, we try to be thoroughly mindful of every detail of our bodily posture and movement. We have a formal and traditional way of entering the meditation hall, walking to our seats, bowing to our cushions, and taking our places. We sit on our cushions according to instructions on seven points of posture that we find in meditation texts throughout Buddhist history. And then we follow the instruction that says, "Take a deep breath, inhale and exhale, rock your body right and left and settle into a steady, immobile sitting position."

Zazen practice is selfless. Its meaning, the enlightenment and liberation of all living beings, is not brought forth by the power of personal effort and is not brought forth by the power of others. We can't do it by ourselves, and nobody else can do it for us. The meaning is realized interactively in the context of our wholehearted effort. As the "Song of the Jewel Mirror Samadhi" says, "Inquiry and response come up together." The meaning arises at the same moment as our devotion to the ceremony. Because the meaning arises simultaneously with the performance of the ceremony, there can be no awareness of the actual meaning separate from the form of the ceremony itself. Therefore, although the meaning of zazen can be realized, it is inconceivable. Because enlightenment is realized right at the same time as the selfless practice of this ritual, it is a ceremony of inconceivable liberation.

The stillness of Buddha's sitting is not merely stillness: it is complete presence in stillness. In such presence, there is not the slightest meddling with what's happening. It is a physical and mental noninterfering with our experience. It is a thorough intimacy with whatever is happening. This is an infinitely flexible stillness that can adjust to the impermanent nature of all things, harmonizing with all situations.

Although this upright stillness is an essential awareness, nevertheless, it is an initiatory awareness. It opens the door to a full understanding of how self and other dependently coproduce each other. This understanding of the interdependent arising of all beings is the samadhi of all buddhas. In this realm of awareness, the culmination of Zen practice, that is, the liberation of all beings, is realized.

Zazen is completely free: it is formless and no person or school owns it. Yet the most essential and intimate aspect of training in the formless zazen of the buddha ancestors occurs in the realm of form. In this regard, I deeply appreciate how the forms of sitting practice can help us develop wisdom and compassion.

Green Dragon Temple
Green Gulch Farm
Muir Beach, California
Summer 1997

THREE

✺

A Field Far Beyond Form
and Emptiness

One day Yantou shouted at his dharma brother Xuefeng, "Haven't you heard that what comes in through the front gate is not the family jewels?"

Xuefeng asked, "Then how should I practice?"

Yantou said, "If you want to propagate the great way, let each point of the teaching flow out from your breast and cover heaven and earth for me." At these words, Xuefeng was greatly enlightened.[1]

Everything can be a family jewel if one is calm and ready and cultivates the field of our experience. Then one can catch things as they first arise. One can witness one's life as it is created. One may think that if one understands, then one will be able to create; but the other way around may be more accurate: if one witnesses one's creation, one will understand. If one's body-mind is well worked and comfortable, one can be present and attend its creation. As Suzuki Roshi said, unless we know the origin of our effort, we don't actually understand our effort. We have to understand the origin of what we are doing here in our lives, in our practice. Unless we do this groundwork of caring for the ordinary details of our lives, we are simply not walking on the ground. This work is not at all glamorous, yet it develops the wondrous mind that appreciates all life. As an old saying goes, "Behind every jewel are three thousand sweating workhorses."

In our sitting practice, we cultivate calmness. We cultivate alert, flexible, and stable bodies and minds, and this cultivation is a nurturing activity, a mothering activity. When this mothering activity is thorough, a new growth of practice sprouts. We can see it and enjoy it. An experienced gardener told me that after a field is prepared, it's very important to take care of the two inches of air above the ground. In meditation, after we take care of the ground of consciousness, we must also care for the living space just above the surface of this nurtured, stabilized consciousness. The lotus sprouts in that two inches. It's very important to catch that first thought-sprout just as it pops up.

The Tang poet Wang Wei said,

I follow the stream to the source.

I sit there and watch for the moment

when the clouds crop up.[2]

If something comes up and we miss the beginning, we cannot fully appreciate the later growth. We have missed the moment of its connection with its ground source. On the other hand, when we witness the birth of a thing, we deeply appreciate and nurture it.

It's the same for the birth of a child. If the mother has been drugged and can't see the baby when he or she first emerges, or if the baby is taken from her immediately, it undermines the formation of the early mother-child bond. It's true for fathers, too. For a long time, fathers did not directly witness the delivery of their babies. Lately, however, men are being allowed to attend the birth of their children. The difference between being there when the baby first comes out and being there just a few minutes later is momentous. It has been found that when a father forms an early nurturing bond with his child, the incidence of incest is much lower. Our reverence and appreciation for life is deepened when we witness its birth.

Seeing the first little bump of my daughter as she was coming out of her mother, after I'd been there for nine months of pregnancy and twenty-three hours of labor, was vitally important to me. I saw the bump and I followed its curve and imagined the size of the head. But the shape of her head as it first appeared was not the shape that it would actually be. There is a good deal of pressure on the head at the opening, so what appears is just the little bulge at the top of the head. Therefore, I thought her head was going to be about the size of a grapefruit. A much, much bigger head came out, about the size of a pumpkin! And I laughed when I saw this huge head come out: a huge head with a calm, alert buddha-face. Ever since that moment, I have deeply appreciated and been devoted to that person. These feelings might have arisen in me even if I had not been present at her birth, but I feel that they were much enhanced by my witnessing her birth, by seeing her as she first appeared.

Fearlessness also comes from the work of attending to and nurturing the ground of our experience. One Zen teacher asked, "Who can untie the bell string around the tiger's neck?" He then answered himself, "The one who tied it can untie it." That person isn't afraid of the tiger, because he knows the tiger and has been intimate with her from the time she was a cub.

When I was a little boy, I was afraid of dogs. I was not afraid of puppies: I was afraid of full-grown dogs. They didn't even have to be very big dogs—just full-grown. The dogs seemed to know that I was afraid, and they chased me all over the neighborhood. Then a German shepherd puppy named Mike came to live in my own house. I wasn't afraid of this German shepherd: he was a cute little guy. He grew and grew and grew until he weighed 115 pounds. As he grew, he also got those male hormones. He became a ferocious dog—much bigger than any dog who had ever chased me. But I wasn't afraid of him, because he had been my puppy. My friends were scared to death of him, and I would tease them by saying, "It's all right, he won't hurt you—if you don't move." So if we know the origins of our lives and of all things, we won't be afraid of anything and we will appreciate everything.

How can I be there when my life arises? It is basic hard work: nurturing, turning, mixing, composting, smoothing the ground of my being and watching it very carefully by being upright and staying awake.

In practicing being upright, one may sometimes have difficulty staying awake. One of the ways one may try to stay awake is by getting angry at not being awake. In such a case, the nurturing approach would be to try to develop friendliness toward one's sleepiness and even friendliness toward one's anger. Anger at not being concentrated agitates one further. But friendliness toward any state calms. On the one hand, one may talk about being alert and concentrated on one's experience of body and mind and, on the other hand, one may speak of just being friendly to whatever happens. Being friendly to whatever is happening is actually another way to concentrate.

This friendly, awake, stable, and supple mind is not simply insight into the true origin of things but is also the enactment of the total vitality of life and death. The great Master Zhaozhou challenged us to be this way.

A monk once asked Zhaozhou, "What's the difference between me and you?"

Zhaozhou said, "I use the twenty-four hours; you are used by the twenty-four hours."

Zhaozhou challenges us to practice the yoga of being upright, awake, and friendly throughout the twenty-four hours, to use the opportunity that is offered by each thought, each breath. This is the way to live without hindering our vitality or being driven by it.

This kind and nurturing way of practice is sometimes called the gate of cultivation. We practice the gate of cultivation by completely embracing each breath, alert for the way to totally exert our breath and be totally exerted by it. In this realm of total exertion, teachings appear in ordinary things, and Zhaozhou's challenge to use the twenty-four hours of daily life is realized. Then we understand the ancestors' words, "This very mind is Buddha." This meticulous attention to the details of our experience is the hallmark of our particular stream of Zen and is the key that opens the heart teaching of our lineage: "Form itself is emptiness; emptiness itself is form." The same is true of all dharmas. Our very feelings, ideas, emotions, and awareness are not different from absolute emptiness, the origin of all beings.

The gate of cultivation that I have been discussing is sometimes described as going from ordinariness to awakening. In addition to this gate, we sometimes speak of the natural, or spontaneous, gate, which is described as coming from awakening into ordinariness. Now we may be ready to open and discuss this other gate. To do so, I'll start by retelling a modern Zen koan about coming from awakening into ordinariness. I heard this story from Suzuki Roshi not long before he died. It is the story of a little eight- or ten-year-old monk named Oka-sotan. He grew up to be a great teacher. When he was a little boy at the monastery, he was sent to the store to buy some pickles for dinner. On the way to the store, he stopped to gaze at one of those colorful woodblock prints that were used in those days to advertise kabuki theater and circuses. He stopped for some time—we don't know how long—and, when he heard the bell for evening service, which just precedes dinner, he ran very quickly to the store.

He said to the storekeeper, "Give 'em to me!"

The man said, "What?"

Oka-sotan said, "The pickles!" The man gave him the pickles, and he ran back toward the monastery. But before he got there, he realized that he had forgotten his hat.

So he ran back to the store and said to the man,

"Give it to me!"

The man said, "What?"

He said, "My hat!" and the man said, "It's on your head." Little Oka-sotan ran back to the monastery. End of story.

This sounds like my life: I might do something like that. It is the ordinary stuff that happens to people. The reason it is a koan is because I am telling you it is a koan. I am telling you it is a koan because it has been a koan for me. It has been a jewel for me—not just because it is a nice story about a great Zen master but because, after Suzuki Roshi told the story, he said, "He was a very good boy." He was a very good boy. He was Buddha. Not just because he grew up to be a big buddha, but because he was a little buddha. Can you see Buddha in that story?

After telling you this story, I offer these words of caution about studying koans, the oral tradition of Zen Buddhism. The context of koan study is total exertion. Our ancestor Dongshan Liangjie said,

If you're excited, it becomes a pitfall.

If you miss it, you fall into retrospective hesitation.[3]

If you study before taking good care of yourself, before you are concentrated and ready, an awakening may come, but this is just an idea of buddha. The buddha you find when you are not ready comes through the front gate. The buddha that comes in the front gate is an illusion, it is *mara*. It is just a picture of buddha. It is not outside the mind. One Zen master said, "If you meet buddha on the road, kill it." This means, kill the idea that buddha is something outside yourself. When you are calm and ready, buddha doesn't come through the front gate, and you will understand this story from your own life, because you are just as stupid as this boy and also just as good. This is a koan for you to study when you have been very friendly to everything that happens to you for a moment, for a day, for a week. If you try it and you get excited and stop taking care of yourself, then stop studying the koan and go back to caring for yourself. Otherwise, you will just be dreaming that you realize why Oka-sotan is a good boy, a very good boy.

Green Dragon Temple
Green Gulch Farm
Muir Beach, California
Fall 1984

FOUR

✹

Sitting in the Heart of Suffering

It has been said that all the buddhas and ancestors are sitting at the heart of all the worlds of suffering. This is the way they develop their unshakable vow to drop body and mind, and thus save all sentient beings.

Depending on how we conduct our lives, we find ourselves in one of a variety of forms of existence. Of course, these varieties are endless, but there are six major categories, called the six worlds. These worlds, which we create for ourselves, have names we have given them: the human realm; the realm of divine bliss; the hell realm of extreme torment and isolation; the insatiable realm of the hungry ghosts; the animal realm of fear; and the realm of the fighting gods.

The human realm is the center of gravity of the other five. As human beings, we tend to return here. *Jambudvipa*, which in Sanskrit means "apple-rose island," is in the very heart of the human realm. This is where we are right now. It is the place where we feel connection with all forms of suffering.

Here in *Jambudvipa*, the heart of suffering, all manifestations of suffering are close at hand, from the most gross to the most subtle. When you are in the realm of bliss, it is difficult to empathize with extreme torment and isolation. When you are in a state of great torment, it is hard to appreciate bliss. But at the center of this range of suffering, we can sense the suffering that is present within blissful experience, within torment, within insatiability, within fear and numbness, and within power seeking.

The human realm may be described basically as dissatisfaction, the frustration of all our desires and strivings. Things just aren't quite the way we want them to be, and yet it is only in this realm that we have the possibility of seeing things just the way they are. There is no point in looking to another realm for comfort. The only real comfort is to be found by settling in right here and now.

Our sitting practice is this settling in and making ourselves at home at the heart of all sentient beings. How do we do this? Actually, it's a simple practice. There is nothing to do, because we are already at this place, but, because of our accumulated opinions, philosophies, and striving human nature, we are obstructed from this simple practice of paying attention to what is right under our feet at this very moment. Great effort is required to be free of our ideas about effort. It takes courage to give up our personal views and to attend to our lives, just as they are.

One description of this process that I find very helpful is given by the Tang dynasty Chinese Buddhist poet Wang Wei:

In my middle years I became fond of the way.

I make my home in the foothills of South Mountain.

When the spirit moves me, I go off by myself

to see things that I alone must see.

I follow the stream to the source.

I sit there and watch for the moment when the

clouds crop up.

Or I may meet a woodsman,

And we laugh and talk and forget about going home.[1]

At first, sitting meditation is a settling down and a retiring to the foothills. Then, when the spirit moves us, when something happens, we follow the stream to the source: the heart of all sentient beings. We sit still and observe the time when the clouds crop up. To be present at this moment is to witness both the inevitability of thought and its illusory nature. This is the birth of compassion: when we observe the production of phenomena and understand their source.

The source of the stream of experience is completely calm and serene. Still, something will crop up. For example, when Kishizawa Ian, Suzuki Roshi's second teacher, was a young monk, he was sitting in meditation on a rainy day and heard the sound of a distant waterfall. Then the wooden *han* was struck. He went to his teacher and asked, "What is the place where the sound of the rain, the waterfall, and the *han* meet?"

His teacher replied, "True eternity still flows."

And then he asked, "What is this true eternity that still flows?"

"It is like a bright mirror, permanently smooth," said his teacher.

"Is there anything beyond this?" asked the young monk.

"Yes," responded his teacher.

"What is beyond this?" inquired the young monk.

And his teacher replied, "Break the mirror. Come, and I'll meet you."[2]

When we are at this source, sitting completely still, all buddhas and sentient beings are there with us. Then, because we are alive, this calm mirror experience breaks, and clouds of thinking crop up. At this point, we don't have to think, Now I must be compassionate. Just being willing to give up great calm and to become involved again in particular thoughts is compassion. In this way, we knowingly and willingly re-enter the world of confusion and suffering.

Clouds crop up at the source of all thought. At that point, we feel connection with all the different varieties of suffering. We sit calmly without fear. We are open and at ease. We could stand up from our sitting and walk to hell, walk to heaven, or walk to the animal realm. We could also welcome them if they came to us. From this place, compassion is not dualistic: we don't do it and we cannot stop it. Our body interacts fearlessly with all forms of suffering. This does not mean that the fear does not exist—or that it does exist. It means that we are open to all varieties of fear, so that the forces around us are balanced. We do not have more friends in heaven than we have in hell. If we have too many friends in heaven and not enough in hell, then there will be fear. So we can look at the community we live in. Do we know more people in heaven than in hell? If we do, we are not truly calm. If we observe our own bodies and minds as we are sitting, and find that we have more friends in heaven than in hell, or more friends in hell than in heaven, we have not yet realized the calm of Buddha's mind. Whenever our minds are completely open and we are not controlling what we are exposed to, our bodies and minds can sit still, in the heart of all suffering beings. That is all we have to do. Everything else will take care of itself.

In our basic instructions for upright sitting, we say, "Don't lean to the right or to the left. Don't lean forward or backward." We harmonize body and mind. This is downright sitting.

Buddha asked his ordained disciples to beg for their food from house to house, without prejudice toward the rich or the poor. Mahakasyapa, the first ancestor in our lineage, preferred to beg only in the poor neighborhoods. Buddha told him that he should not beg just from the poor, even though that was his tendency.

So we have tendencies to lean this way or that way, forward or backward, and occasionally our teachers may adjust our posture and show us what it feels like to be in the middle. We tend to go back to the way we were, until we find out that being off balance is painful. That is why sitting is very good. If we are off center and sit long enough, we will find out that it doesn't work. The most comfortable way is upright sitting, where we don't emphasize one direction more than any other. Eventually our own experience will bring us back to the middle—if we sit again and again. But if we are not paying attention to our experience, we may not be able to learn from and it thus not be able to and find our way home.

I personally need to sit every day. Although I have

been sitting for a while, it is still difficult for me. When I get up in the morning, I am often aching and slow to get going. I take this sore, resistant body, and I put it on a black cushion. As I stretch and settle into the sitting position, the resistance falls away. If I didn't do that, then later in the day, I would not be ready for the other kinds of suffering that arise. But if I can let this body settle into itself, then it is empty and open, and I'm ready to meet all of you.

It's like bamboo in the falling snow. Snow piles up on the leaves, and the bamboo bends. It bends and bends and bends. It keeps bending all the way down until finally the snow drops off and the branches spring back. We have to experience and accept our share of suffering every day, and then it can drop away, leaving us ready to live.

When I look at the picture on the wall of our compassionate teacher, Suzuki Roshi, I feel that he is inviting all of us to come and sit with him. This sitting is a great joy for all the buddhas and ancestors. They are connected to us; they are always with us. We don't just sit with them. We also stand up and walk, bringing the heart of suffering into all the activities of our daily lives. Then true eternity flows, wherever we are. Come back to sit. Please come back, every day.

Green Dragon Temple
Green Gulch Farm
Muir Beach, California
Spring 1985

FIVE

✸

The Five *Skandhas*

Once there was a man, and his name was Shakyamuni. He woke up at some point and became very happy; he became very helpful to all other living beings. We are still practicing his way. He talked a lot, to get his disciples interested in life. He wanted them to notice their lives.

I have said it before, and I'll keep on saying it: Buddha did not say that life as such is frustrating and painful. Many people think that he did say that, but he didn't. Actually, his enlightened view was that life is incomparable, indescribable, beyond all human evaluation: he might have said, Wow! Wonderful, wonderful! It's wonderful not only for me, but for everybody! He tried to convey his enthusiasm for the awakened life to everyone. He taught that life is not necessarily painful; it is painful only under certain conditions. He called those conditions craving and clinging, and this is what I would like to bring to our attention today.

When Shakyamuni Buddha was seven days old, according to tradition, he lost his mother. (Many of the great teachers, from many spiritual disciplines, have lost their parents at an early age.) Buddha was a bright child; he noticed that he had lost his mother, even though she was quickly replaced by a loving aunt, and he grew up in very pleasant circumstances. Partly, I think, because of that initial tragedy, Buddha's father made every effort to shield him from contact with any kind of unpleasantness. I agree with that attitude. I think that children should be given as much love and nourishment and protection from pain as possible, and then they may grow up to be strong and sensitive, and be able to see what Shakyamuni saw when he grew up: namely, that everybody suffers, gets sick, grows old, and dies. He noticed that.

He also noticed that, even though everyone knows that they will get sick, grow old, and die—guess what? They find the same process in others disgusting. Strange, isn't it? Even Shakyamuni was disgusted with this process in others. However, he also felt ashamed of his disgust at a normal process that everyone must undergo. So, having lost his mother, having been raised with love and comfort, being very sensitive, and recognizing his own disgust at disease, decay, and death, he made a great renunciation. He left his privileged social sphere and entered a very different one. There he immersed himself in sickness, old age, and death, and in his shame about being disgusted by those characteristics in others.

Now this story can be understood as a biography, and it can also be seen as a psychological metaphor. We have all experienced a time of knowing the bliss of oneness, and we have all lost it. We all lose that radical innocence. When we realize our loss, then we can begin to search for a way back to oneness.

But the happiness we experienced when we were

very young was not known consciously. It is a joy too complete to recognize itself. So part of our necessary development as human beings is not only to have a great, loving, blissful heart, but also to know it, to recognize it fully. When we first experienced this happiness, as babies, it was a dark, unconscious bliss. Our assignment in life, as human beings, is to find again—through the suffering of separation, through the yearning for union—that bliss. Buddha teaches that through illuminating this pain, this loss, this broken heart from which everything begins, we can become free.

I have often been struck by the fact that the first noble truth, that there is suffering, which Buddha encouraged us to contemplate, is not very attractive. Wouldn't it be more pleasant to meditate upon the vastness of consciousness or a golden buddha? But our first instructions from Buddha were to look at something rather unattractive: namely, the origin of suffering.

This reminds me of an old joke. One evening two men were standing on a sidewalk, looking down into the gutter under a streetlight. A police officer came up to them and said, "What are you guys doing?"

One of the men replied, "We're looking for his watch."

"Oh, did you drop it here?" said the police officer.

The other man answered, "No, I dropped it up the street, but the light's better here."

We've lost our watches and we usually like to look for them where there is already a nice, bright light. For most of us, suffering and frustration exist in darkness, without nice lights, or beautiful golden auras, or nice songs, or beautiful people saying, "Come on! Look right here." Our watches are actually in the silent, intimidating, dark places. We can scout around in some really nice locations in our psyches—but that may not be where our watches are or our . . . What was it that we lost? The happiness of being alive?

As I mentioned before, Buddha did not say that life as such is frustrating. In Sanskrit, he said, *Upadana panca skandha dukkha. Upadana* means "clinging." *Panca* means "five." *Skandha* means "aggregate"; and *dukkha* means "suffering" or "frustration." So, clinging to the five aggregates—that's the definition of *dukkha:* that's our suffering. Clinging to the five aggregates is really the only problem in life. If you don't cling to the five aggregates, life is just life.

The first of the five aggregates is form, or *rupa,* in Sanskrit. There are ten types of form. There are the five sense fields: color, sound, smell, taste, and touch. Then there are the five sense capacities, sometimes called sense organs: eye organ, ear organ, nose organ, tongue organ, and body organ. The organs are sensitive to and respond to the phenomena called sense fields. The eye organ is something located in a living being that is sensitive to and responds to color. All life is physically based: there are no living beings which do not respond to physicality, to the first aggregate.

The next aggregate is *vedana,* which means "feeling" or "sensation." There are three kinds of sensation: feeling

38

pain, feeling pleasure, and being confused about just what one is feeling. This evaluative function is present in every experience.

The third one is called perception, or *samjna*. This is a process by which an image of an object of awareness is brought into contact with consciousness.

The next aggregate, *samskara*, which means "formations," is composed of many different elements. Here you will find anger, confusion, lust, faith, concentration, diligence, shame, shamelessness, fear of blame—and the many, many other psychological processes. These processes have a tendency to condition the other *skandhas*. They influence the form aggregate, the feeling aggregate, and the conception aggregate. They also modify the fifth aggregate, which is *vijnana*, the aggregate of consciousness, or cognition.

Those are the five. All living beings are just those five aggregates. No living beings have any type of experience outside of these five types. A moment of life is composed of these five aggregates, these five sources. Our practice is to become familiar with these five groupings, with what they really are, with how they happen, and with how they collaborate to conjure up this wonderful event called life.

Remember, Buddha didn't say that these five processes are frustrating and painful. These five are life. Frustration is clinging to these five things. Trying to cling to these five things is like trying to cling to five people: five teenagers, five 3-year-olds, or five drunken football players. It's like trying to control five vital, constantly changing, dynamic entities. It is a frustrating experience. These five things are happening every moment: all five, with total creative energy, fully realizing themselves instantly. Then they go away and instantaneously five others appear. The basic problem in life is that we try to control something that we never have the slightest chance of controlling. What we become, if we can just let the *skandhas* happen, is beyond "good" or "bad," beyond pain or pleasure. We become life.

I was driving down the Green Gulch entrance road some years ago, when Jerry Brown was still governor, and I heard an interview with him on the radio. He said something like, "I'm just a Ping-Pong ball on the top of a fountain." Can you picture a fountain going up with a Ping-Pong ball bouncing around on top of it? I thought to myself, That's pretty good! It's a good example of what Buddha called self-clinging. What the governor was describing is very close to our definition of suffering. The Ping-Pong ball is extra; it's an illusion. Life is actually just a fountain. There is no Ping-Pong ball on top. If you take a snapshot of the top of the fountain, just the gush of water forming the top surface—that's a moment of life. There is no Ping-Pong ball on top, no "self" in addition to the flow of the five *skandhas*.

We try to grab hold of the fountain. We can't. We can disturb it, but if we try to grasp it we are going to be frustrated.

Human beings have the audacity to dream of controlling something that is beyond control. This is the fundamental definition of suffering, and it is the only problem in life. *Upadana panca skandha dukkha.* The fountain is not the problem. It's the attempt to control the fountain that brings about problems. Human beings are not good at controlling themselves or their experiences.

The problem doesn't stop there: it gets worse. Not only do we try to control ourselves, we also try to control others, who are also beyond control. I tried for many years to control Zen students, but they resist control. So I gave up some years ago.

We are not good at controlling life, but we are fairly proficient at "ordering." Ordering is not the same as controlling. For example, cleaning your desk: that's not a controlling act. While you are trying to get the desk cleared, the telephone may ring; your children may come and climb on you; a lamp may fall on you; and you may forget, in the middle of the clearing away, that you wanted to do it in the first place. These things may happen. These are matters of control. But if you want to clean off your desk, someday you may be able to accomplish it. Then you can take a book or a piece of paper and put it on your desk. On the book or piece of paper might be the words, *Upadana panca skandha dukkha.* Just look at it. What's your life about?

I put quite a bit of effort into order, and I try to put almost no effort into control. If I put a lot of effort into ordering, I realize even more deeply what a waste of time control is. For example, every morning I sit in my seat and I simply try to sit still. I don't try to control myself into sitting still; I try to sit still as an ordering activity. I can't actually control myself into sitting still. I can't make myself sit still. The only way I can sit still is if everybody in the universe makes me sit still. All of us together are perfectly in control of me. All of you, plus everyone else in the universe, is completely in control of me. What I am is actually what everything has made. In that sense, each of us is under control. The entire cosmos is controlling us, but individually, we cannot control anything.

The more still I sit, the more deeply I realize that I never can sit still. Also, I realize ever more deeply that I always have been sitting still, in the sense of all living beings making me sit still at every moment. Every moment, I am completely still; but the kind of stillness that I *try* to achieve, I can never accomplish. By ordering my life, I realize that control is a wasted effort. Ordering also facilitates, or supports, my realization of what I am good at: I'm good at being me. Moment by moment, I am a fountain, I am spontaneous creativity. I am not in control of this creativity, but I am its site: pure, universally connected creativity. Each one of us is such a site. Each one of us is a fountain of the universe. Each one of us is a place where the universe is expressing itself as a living location. If I order my life, then I can see the fountain; or, not *see* it so much as *be* it (because there is no "person" here looking at a fountain). Just being a fountain, there is just the life of the fountain; there is just life. No one watches life: life includes the "observers."

I want to give you an example of how to study with one of those *skandhas*. Let's take the form aggregate.

What we find here is a psycho-physical process. Buddhas wake up in the midst of psycho-physical processes. Another way of saying it is that buddhas wake up in the midst of delusion. Illusions are conjured up by psycho-physical processes. We live in illusions; we wake up in the middle of that process of illusion. We don't wake up in the middle of enlightenment, or in the middle of empty space. What we wake up about and in and through is delusion. That's the way we wake up; that's our home; that's our food. The five *skandhas*, the five aggregates, that is where we wake up.

For example, Buddha asks, "Why do we say 'body'? We are affected, therefore we say 'body.'" That is what he means by "body." Body is not a thing. Once I said, "Body is that which is affected," and someone pointed out that this was not a good way of phrasing it. It is not as though there were a thing that is affected; it's not a body with arms, legs, and torso that is affected. What I move around in time and space is not what Buddha meant by "body." This is not a living body. The experience of being affected is not bodily experience. It's conceptual experience.

Often we regard a concept as our bodies. We run up and down hills, swim in the ocean, and so on, and what we are really doing is taking our concepts, putting them into situations, and working the concepts.

We're hungry for physical experience, and not because we aren't having experiences, but because we are not aware of our physical experiences.

So the problem lies in the confusion between conceptual experience of the body and actual bodily experience. In fact, arms and legs are concepts; they are not physical entities. Objectively, *physicality* means "a composition of the four great elements." Subjectively, *physicality* means "being affected." The body is actually a location where one is affected.

How? Being affected by colors, sounds, smells, and flavors. Being affected by heat, being affected by cold, being affected by pressure, hard and soft, rough and smooth: this is the body. To discover the body, begin by trying to find a physical experience that is actually physical, not just conceptual. Next, notice the conceptual experience of the body; and finally, make an effort to clearly distinguish between the two.

Can you imagine living in the world on the basis of how you are affected physically, rather than negotiating concepts such as "arms" and "legs" through space and time? Can you imagine shifting your orientation so that you're living from how you are affected?

When it's time to move, I may be afraid to let go of body concepts. I may think, How will I get down the stairs? How will I get food into my mouth? Don't worry. All these body concepts will still keep coming up: concepts of spoon, hand, oatmeal, mouth, and distance from mouth to spoon. So I will still be able to eat and walk and so on. But can I shift over to find out what it is like to live with the whole body?

This shift is supported by ordering my life, for example, deciding that for the next ten minutes, I am going to just sit here; or that for the next ten minutes, I am going to walk very slowly, not doing anything fancy. I am going to be in a situation where I will feel safe, and I am going to try to understand what Buddha means when he says that the body is "being affected." In that way, I order my life so that I make a time and a space for studying each of these *skandhas*. We all can spend five or ten minutes asking ourselves, What kinds of feelings are happening? Am I having a pleasurable feeling or a painful feeling? We need to order our lives so that we can actually examine the elements of our experience. Being "Buddha" is being greatly awakened in the midst of delusion, being awake in the dance of these five *skandas*. Here is an example of what it is like to look, an example of a little awakening.

My daughter had a friend staying over one night. When her friend's mother came, the friend went and sat on her lap. My daughter felt that her friend was intentionally excluding her by expressing affection for her mother. After her friend had left, my daughter went to her own mom and told her how she had felt excluded by her friend. Then she climbed on my lap, at which her mother said, "Are you intentionally trying to exclude me?" She replied, "No, I'm just hugging my dad." My daughter then realized that being affectionate to a mom or dad is not necessarily excluding others from one's affections. So she said, "Okay, I'll give her another chance. I'll give her one more day. I'll watch her."

At school the next day, she watched her friend throughout the day. Returning home, she said, "I noticed that I was getting angry at her because of the way I was thinking. The way I was thinking about her made me angry."

This is an example of a little insight, a little awakening that can happen when you turn around and look at your feelings, concepts, and so on; look at how they work, what they do. Even a child can do it, but you have to order your life with some intention, such as, "Okay, I'll give her another chance. I'll look tomorrow." That's an ordering attitude.

We can order our lives to look at ourselves. We can learn that whenever we're frustrated, it comes from trying to cling to the ungraspable, uncontrollable activity of our lives. If we are just the spontaneous, uncontrollable activity, there's no frustration. Then we will not try to control other living creatures, and we will not cause them any harm.

This is Shakyamuni Buddha's ancient teaching on how to just be here. From here, we can move forward to benefit all living beings.

Beginner's Mind Temple
The City Center
San Francisco, California
Spring 1988

SIX

※

Just Sitting

The teaching of thusness has been intimately communicated by buddhas and ancestors. The meaning of this practice of suchness is not in words, and yet it responds to our energy, it responds to our effort. It comes forth and meets us. We sit here and the blue jays sing it to us, the stream sings it to us, because we come and listen. This is our practice of sitting, just sitting. It is a themeless meditation, a seamless meditation. It has no form, no beginning, and no end, and it pervades every-thing completely. It leaves no traces, and if I try to trace it, it's not that I trace it, but that it generously and compassionately responds to my tracing, to my speaking, and to your listening.

Shakyamuni Buddha transmitted the teaching of thusness. He said the following:

"Please train yourselves thus: In the seen, there will be just the seen. In the heard, there will be just the heard. In the sensed, there will be just the sensed. In the cognized, there will be just the cognized. When for you, in the seen there is just the seen, in the heard just the heard, in the sensed just the sensed, in the cognized just the cognized, then you will not identify with the seen, and so on. And if you do not identify with them, you will not be located in them; if you are not located in them, there

47

will be no here, no there, or in-between. And this will be the end of suffering."[1]

This is themeless meditation. It is seamless meditation. There is no seam between you and the heard: there is just the heard. No seam: only the heard and the seen and the imagined. This is having no object of thought.

Shakyamuni Buddha also said, "If you approach the five *skandhas*, if you approach colors or sounds, or if they approach you, this is misery."

Approaching colors is not just the colors being the colors, but you approaching them. This is misery. Approaching feelings, approaching perceptions, approaching emotions, approaching consciousness, making these approaches, or being approached by these phenomena: this is misery. But if we do not approach these phenomena, if there is no seam between them and us, then these very same *skandhas*, these very same colors and sounds, are bliss. We can see the roots of the Zen tradition of objectless meditation in this teaching of Buddha.

When the twenty-first ancestor Vasubandhu was talking with Jayata, the ancestor Jayata said,

"I don't seek enlightenment, nor am I deluded. I don't worship Buddha, nor am I disrespectful. I don't sit for long periods, nor am I lazy. I don't eat only once a day, nor am I a glutton. I am not contented, nor am I greedy. When the mind does not seek anything, this is called the way."[2]

Hearing this, Vasubandhu realized the undefiled knowledge. Hearing this. Now those words are gone. What were they about? Can you hear the spirit of enlightenment, can you smell and taste the spirit of enlightenment in those words? Does it sound familiar? Does it sound like your school song?

After Vasubandhu had realized the undefiled knowledge, he taught his successor, Manorhita. Manorhita asked Vasubandhu, "What is the enlightenment of the buddhas?" Vasubandhu said, "It is the original nature of mind." Manorhita asked, "What is the original nature of mind?"

Vasubandhu said, "The emptiness of the sense organs, the sense consciousness, and the sense fields." Hearing this, Manorhita was enlightened.[3] What are you hearing?

The realization of just conception is the truth, the teaching, the enlightenment of the sages. For the mind to stop on just conception is the way Buddha functions. Vasubandhu does not deny a level of perceptual experience where there is no sense of self and no self-clinging. However, this level is unknown to you in your daily life. The level of your normal experience, where you know things clearly, is concepts. In the practice of sitting, of awareness of body and breath, what you are aware of at the level of knowing is a concept, or a beautiful string of concepts, of the body. If the mind can realize just the concept of body, your work is done. There is direct or immediate bodily experience, and it is from this immediate bodily experience that the conceptual experience of body is created. Just sitting practice is just the mind terminating on the concept of sitting, on the concept of the body and the mind and the breath, sitting.

I looked up the word *just* in the dictionary. In the term *shikantaza*, the word *shikan* is sometimes translated as "just," or "only." *Ta* means "hit," and *za* means "sit." It literal-ly means "hit sitting," but the *ta* really intensifies "sitting." So it means "sitting." *Shikan* means "just," but it also means "by all means do it," or "get on with it." It has been translated into English as "just," or "only," and although that wasn't necessarily the meaning of the original Chinese, the English word *just* is kind of a wonderful word. As an adjective, *just* means "honorable," "fair," as in "just in one's dealings." It means "consistent with that which is morally right, fair, and equitable." It means "properly due," or "merited," as in the phrase *just desserts.* There is a specialty bakery in San Francisco called Just Desserts. *Just desserts* means "proper retribution for what you've done," and it also means "specializing in or concentrating on after-dinner sweets." It also means "honorable after-dinner sweets." The people at Just Desserts have a very good reputation in two ways: first, their reputation for their tasty desserts, and second is their reputation for their moral conduct.

Our sitting is a kind of just dessert. *Just* also means "valid within the law, legitimate, suitable, or fitting." It means "sound, well-founded." It means "exact, accurate." It means "upright before God, righteous, upright before the truth."

Live "just." Just concept, just sitting, just the heard in the heard, just the seen in the seen. Upright hearing, righteous hearing, exact hearing, accurate hearing, sound hearing, hearing in accordance with the law, honorable hear-ing. *Just* is a big word in Buddhism. It's all over the place, everywhere fitting just exactly right with what's happening.

That's the sitting we do: perfectly settled right on itself.

A friend of mine was waiting for the Fillmore bus in San Francisco, and an old man was also there waiting for the bus, an old black man. My friend got into a conversation with him, and he told her that he was one hundred years old. Of course, she asked him, "How did you get to be so old?" He quoted from the Bible: "Not a thing will I withhold from you if you stand upright before me."

You do your part: you put the "just sitting" out there. That's your job. You just sit. That's your energy, coming right down on your energy; precisely, exactly, honorably you, upright you, being your experience. And you will get a response called enlightenment. It's already there, completely pervading you already: you just have to put a little energy forward in order to realize it. But it's not exactly a little energy, or a lot of energy, but just the energy of this moment, whatever it is. That's why you don't need anything else but what you've got. You don't need to be more awake or less awake. You don't need to have more food or less food than you already have. You just need to be just this. This is your upright, honorable self that you have right here. You've got to celebrate it, you've got to be there for it.

What I'm saying here is just reminding you of what you already know, what you already intend. Mostly, what I will be doing besides reminding you will be simply adjusting you, just "justing" you. That's all. That's all I can do. I'm not correcting you, I'm adjusting you. Of course, I can't really adjust you: you're already adjusted. But sometimes I may feel that you'd look a little more "just" if you sat like this, rather than like that. If I see your mudra over here, I may think, You'd be a little bit more just if it were over there. Of course, this way is just, too, but still, I may adjust it over there. It's just my aesthetic opinion. It's just my personal adjustment for you.

I try to steer clear of any kind of judgment in the adjustment: I just adjust. And then it's for you not to think about being judged, but rather whether you feel more just after the adjustment. At first, you may feel sometimes, Gee, this is wacko. I feel kind of off. I thought I was sitting upright, but now I feel like I'm leaning somewhat. Maybe in that doubt that you feel after a postural adjustment or after a verbal adjustment, in the reorientation that you experience at that point, even though it may be sort of a surprise and you may wonder what's going on, you will be reminded of something that you heard before about the buddha way. As Vasubandhu said, "I don't seek enlightenment, nor am I deluded." I'm not right or wrong. I'm in some place that's beyond hearing and seeing. So if you are in the realm of hearing and seeing, and you get adjusted into the space that's beyond hearing and seeing, there may be a slight disorientation for a while. Suddenly, you're living someplace where you can't get a hold of anything.

When you're just sitting, you can't get a hold of anything, because you're just sitting. You're not sitting and getting a hold of something. You're just sitting: you're earnestly doing just that. When you lose that something else that may have given you some orientation—of being here or there or in between—at first you may wonder what's going on. But you might trust that new space, that space where you don't know exactly what's happening. At least, trust it for a little while.

It was like this for Bodhidharma. He didn't have any special teachings for his disciple Huike. He just said, "Outside, have no involvements." That's it! No involvements. "Inside, have no sighing or coughing. With your mind like a wall, thus you enter the way." With your mind like a wall: in other words, just. With your mind just, or your mind thus. Thus you enter the way.[4]

He didn't say much, but that's the teaching for a lifetime, right there. That's all you need: "Outside, have no involvements. Inside, have no sighing or coughing." No sighing, no shrinking away from exactly just this. Inside, no shrinking violet: I can't live up to this experience, it's too much for me! It's too fast, it's too intense, it's too yucky! None of that! Also, no coughing or scoffing. Such as, This is beneath me. I've got better things to do than think this way. There are better birds than blue jays to listen to. Now, woodpeckers are different. They're really interesting. No coughing in the mind, and also no shrinking away. Don't get rid of it, don't shrink away from it. Just, inside, let it be thus: let your experience be like a wall.

We have a traditional meal ritual in Soto Zen. The set of bowls that we use for this ritual is called *oryoki*. *Oryoki* means "just enough equipment," or "bowls that are just enough" to support our lives. At the end of the meal, we lean forward to wash these bowls. This is a time when being tall might be difficult. Somebody who is quite tall is many feet away from his bowl. If you're tall and you wear glasses and you don't have them on, you can't even see your bowl down there, right? So you may have the impulse to get your eyes closer to look: Say, what's happening down there? There are some bowls and food and all kinds of stuff! It's okay if you want to get your face way down there; but keep your back straight. If you bend over, bend over with a straight back. Don't hunch over. It's another "just" type of thing. In other words, be aware of your back. It makes quite a difference, and it's good exercise for your back, too, incidentally. Most of these things happen to be good exercise.

Also, try not to put your elbows on your knees to hold yourself up. Use your back. Leaning on your elbows is kind of friendly, it's true. Well, here I am, I'm working on my bowls, and, you know, what's the problem? It's not really a bad thing to do. But a straight back is very precise. It's more present. When you hunch your back, your consciousness goes. I don't know what happens to it. You can get bent way over without noticing that you're doing it. These little things such as keeping your back straight and being on time, these are about justness, too.

There's a poem called "Love," by George Herbert, which I think is about justness. It's about our uncertainty, our lack of faith, as to whether we can really be just, in all the meanings of *just.*

Love

Love bade me welcome: yet my soul drew back,
Guilty of dust and sin.
But quick-eyed Love, observing me grow slack
From my first entrance in,
Drew nearer to me, sweetly questioning
If I lacked anything.

"A guest," I answered, "worthy to be here":
Love said, "You shall be he."
"I, the unkind, ungrateful? Ah, my dear,
I cannot look on thee."
Love took my hand, and smiling did reply,
"Who made the eyes but I?"

"Truth, Lord; but I have marred them; let my shame
Go where it doth deserve."
"And know you not," said Love, "who bore the blame?"
"My dear, then I will serve."
"You must sit down," said Love, "and taste my meat."
So I did sit and eat.[5]

Zen Mind Temple
Tassajara Zen Mountain Center
Carmel Valley, California
March 23 1989

PART TWO

✹

EMBRACING ALL BEINGS

The Sixteen Great Bodhisattva Precepts

The Three Refuges
I take refuge in buddha.

I take refuge in dharma.

I take refuge in sangha.

The Three Pure Precepts
I vow to embrace and sustain right conduct.

I vow to embrace and sustain all good.

I vow to embrace and sustain all beings.

The Ten Grave Precepts
A disciple of Buddha abstains from killing.

A disciple of Buddha abstains from taking
what is not given.

A disciple of Buddha abstains from misusing sexuality.

A disciple of Buddha abstains from lying.

A disciple of Buddha abstains from intoxicating the
mind or body of self or others.

A disciple of Buddha abstains from speaking
of others' faults.

A disciple of Buddha abstains from praising self
at the expense of others.

A disciple of Buddha abstains from clinging to anything,
even the dharma.
A disciple of Buddha abstains from harboring ill will.
A disciple of Buddha abstains from abusing
the three treasures.

SEVEN

✸

Speaking the Unspoken

Shortly before Dogen Zenji died, he was talking to his close disciple Tettsu Gikai about the method for transmitting the bodhisattva precepts. He said, "Please come closer." And Gikai came over to the edge of his bed and stood by his right side and listened. Dogen Zenji said, "In this present lifetime, there are ten million things that I do not understand concerning the buddhadharma of the Tathagata. However, concerning the buddhadharma, I have the joy of not giving rise to evil views. Depending on the correct dharma, I certainly have correct faith. It is only this fundamental intention that I have taught, nothing else. You should understand this."[1]

Today, I want to talk about my personal search for this fundamental intention that the buddhas teach. I could start when I was about eight years old, sitting in my room by myself, looking out the window. I heard a ringing in my ears and, not knowing what it was, I thought, Is this my conscience? I think something's bothering me. A few years later, as a twelve-year-old, I decided to do what gave me the most gain in my social world, which was to be as outrageous as possible. I got lots of attention from my friends for being a wild boy. Whenever I did anything naughty, they got excited and praised me. I was a hero in my school for causing trouble. Then I met a man, a big man, a strong man, who noticed what I was doing. He loved me and he told me that in his youth he had been just like me. He looked at me and said, "You know, it's actually quite easy to be bad. What's really difficult is to be good." I thought, He knows, and I decided at that time to try to be good.

But I had a lot of problems at that time. I was suffering and anxious about unimportant things, such as how I looked, whether people liked me, and how popular I was at school. I realized that if I could just somehow be kind to everyone, all my problems would drop away. Again I decided, as sincerely as I could, to try to be kind to everyone. However, this decision was made in the quiet of my own room at home, and as soon as I got to school I always forgot.

I continued to forget for a number of years, yet somewhere along the line I read some stories about Zen monks. I heard about the way they conducted their lives. I read about Hakuin Zenji and about Ryokan. When I read their stories, I remembered my childhood vow. When I heard about how these men lived, I said, This is the way I want to be. This is the way to be free of all my problems with people.

I wanted to be like those Zen monks, though I had no idea how. But I thought, Perhaps they're not good just by chance. Maybe they all do some kind of exercise that promotes this kind of compassion. And I found out that what they all do is sit. So I started to sit.

The more I sat and the more I studied, the more wonderful I found this sitting. The more I heard teachings about it, the more grateful I felt to have found this sitting: so simple, so all-consuming, so perfect, and so effective.

I practiced sitting for a number of years, enjoying it very much, but to tell you the truth, I forgot, in a way, my original motivation: to be a compassionate person, to be a good person. I forgot about that and just practiced sitting. Also, to tell you the truth, I didn't hear much teaching about being good and about being compassionate. I didn't hear it at the Zen Center where I practiced, and I didn't hear it from people at other Zen centers either. But it didn't seem to be a problem, because the sitting itself was so all-inclusive and wonderful.

In this practice, there was a strong emphasis on wisdom, on insight. There was a strong emphasis on the fundamental of sitting with no gaining idea; on a practice that has no sign, no stages, no gain, and, fundamentally, no thinking. All these instructions and indications as to the core of sitting, I found totally adorable. It never crossed my mind that people didn't understand—especially that I didn't understand—what they meant.

Then, after practicing for about sixteen years, I received what we call *shiho*, or dharma transmission. In the process, I read at the bottom of the document called the precept vein, *kechimyaku* (those of you who have lay ordination or priest ordination in the Soto school may have read this, too), "It was revealed and affirmed to the teacher Myozen that the precept vein of the bodhisattva is the single cause of the Zen gate."

I was surprised to find that the gate to this signless,

stageless, objectless, gainless, and beautiful practice of sitting is these bodhisattva precepts. I thought, Why haven't I heard this before?

More and more, I'm finding that Zen teachings, Dogen's teachings, confirm that the precepts are essential. Just before he died, Dogen Zenji said to Gikai, "In our teaching, the transmission of the precepts is the most important condition."

I've heard that in other Buddhist traditions, for example the Theravadan tradition, there is a similar pattern. The Theravadan teacher Achaan Chaa said that the buddhadharma is *dana* (giving), *sila* (precepts), and *bhavana* (cultivation, or meditation practice). But when Westerners come to practice, they aren't interested in *dana* and *sila*. They just want to do the *bhavana*, the meditation practice.

I think that during the rise of Zen in the United States, as my life shows, many of us started sitting right away; we were primarily interested in the essential practice of the Zen school, the sitting. We were not explicitly or consciously exposed to the teachings of giving and ethics, the first two *paramitas*. As a result of not being exposed to these fundamental practices, I feel that our understanding—or my understanding—of the fundamental intention of sitting was perhaps not so correct.

There are numerous statements in Zen that assume that we know that the precept vein is fundamental. For example, Master Rujing said that we don't need to recite scriptures, offer incense, practice repentance, and so on. Only sitting is required. And Dogen Zenji taught that in the true dharma, zazen is the straight way to correct transmission. Zazen is all Buddha taught. Zazen includes precept practice. But they are not saying that we shouldn't practice repentance and precepts. They're just trying to show us what these practices really are.

One of the characteristics, and, I feel, the beauty, of Zen, especially as taught by Dogen Zenji, is that it is so strictly the pure, true, and ultimate teaching. But there *is* a provisional teaching also, and if people never have been exposed to the provisional teaching, there is a possibility of misunderstanding the ultimate, true teaching. Some Zen students actually think, Precepts are not important. Even some Zen scholars say that precepts are a distant cousin of the Buddhist practices, that the true Buddhist practices are meditation and insight, and precepts are not so important. Why do they feel that? Partly because when they look at the published teachings on Zen, they don't see much on precepts.

A few years ago, the Tibetan teacher Tara Tulku came to teach at the Zen Center, and he asked me, "In your meditation, what is the object?"

I said, feeling a little embarrassed, "Well, we don't have any object. We practice objectless meditation."

And he said, "Oh. We have that objectless meditation, too, in Vajrayana, but it is the most advanced meditation. Usually practitioners work for many years before they can do objectless meditation."

He also asked me, "What stages are there in your training?"

I said, "Well, in a way, we're mostly concerned with not falling into stages. It's part of our tradition." I told him the story of Seigen Gyoshi going to the sixth ancestor and asking, "How can I avoid falling into steps and stages?"

And the ancestor said, "What have you been practicing?"

Seigen said, "I haven't even been practicing the Four Noble Truths [that is, I haven't even started the beginning practice]."

And the ancestor said, "Well, what stage have you fallen into?"

And Seigen said, "How could I have fallen into a stage if I haven't even practiced the Noble Truths?"[2]

Tara Tulku said, "Wow! That's very advanced, to be working on not even slipping into or clinging to the various stages of meditation." Again I thought, How subtle, how pure Zen is.

Then he said, "Well, I talked to some of your students, and there are certain things about Mahayana Buddhism that they don't seem to know about."

While this teacher was at the Zen Center, many people came up to me and asked about various practices: Why don't we do this? Why don't we do that? In fact, we were doing the things they were asking about, but they hadn't noticed. For example, they said, "Why don't we make offerings to buddhas and bodhisattvas? Why don't we pay homage to buddhas and bodhisattvas?" I'd say, "We do, every time we chant before having a meal." And then they'd say, "Oh."

These things are part of our tradition, but, in fact, people often don't even know it. That's fine, in a way: it's so subtle, they don't even know it. Still, I was concerned. So I thought perhaps it would be good to tell people that we do make bodhisattva vows, that we actually are bodhisattvas, that we do pay homage to buddhas and bodhisattvas, that we make offerings, and that we take refuge in buddha, dharma, and sangha. It's not that these practices are only for other Buddhists who don't know the subtle teachings of Zen.

For many years at the Zen Center I never really noticed that I had taken refuge in buddha, dharma, and sangha. Now I've learned, again from Dogen's mouth and through Dogen's life. As he was dying, what was he doing? The last practice he did was to walk around a pillar upon which he had written, "buddha, dharma, sangha." And he said, "In the beginning, in the middle, and in the end, in your life as you approach death, in death, after death, and as you approach life, always, through all births and deaths, always take refuge in buddha, dharma, sangha."[3] This fundamental practice that all Buddhists do, many Zen students had never even heard about. It was said, but we didn't hear it, because it wasn't emphasized strongly enough. In some way, our sitting practice is so essential that we may feel we can overlook some of these more basic practices.

But are we really practicing zazen in accord with the fundamental intention that Dogen Zenji taught? Do we have correct faith? Is it possible that as we practice the buddhadharma, some evil, upside-down kind of thinking is arising in our minds? I don't say it is or isn't. I just say,

Are we wondering about that?

We always say, "Just sit." But it's pretty hard to understand what that means. Suzuki Roshi once said, "Receiving the precepts is a way to help us understand what it means to just sit." But then I heard a story about a monk asking Dongshan Liangjie, "What about precepts, concentration, and wisdom?" And Dongshan Liangjie replied, "I have no useless furniture in my house."

This, again, is such a beautiful teaching. It means, of course, that the precepts are not separate from zazen. Zazen already includes the precepts, concentration practice, and wisdom. But I think when I first heard that teaching, it allowed me to not study the precepts as thoroughly as I might have if I had heard from the beginning that the precepts are the most fundamental condition of the Zen gate. When I apply myself to the study of precepts, a kind of integrity comes into my sitting, which helps it to be just sitting in its true sense. Without the precepts, I don't think I can understand what it means to just sit.

When the Zen teacher refers to precepts, concentration, and wisdom, saying that we don't have any unnecessary furniture in our house, I think he means that the precepts are not anything extra in our lives. You can't be a good meditator or a good meditation teacher if you don't understand the precepts. These precepts are not a side issue: they are the core of the process of awakening. What has not been emphasized, and what I'm trying to emphasize at Zen Center now, is that although there are no precepts outside Zen, there is also no Zen outside the precepts. Similarly, there are no bodhisattva vows—there is no wish to save all beings—outside zazen, but also there is no zazen outside the wish to save all beings.

Again, after I had practiced for several years, I read Tientung Rujing, Dogen's teacher. Every time before he sat, he would think, Now I sit in order to save all beings. And he encouraged us to practice in this way. Somehow, before I read Tientung Rujing, I hadn't really deeply heard this teaching. This omission may have been a skillful device in the early transmission of Zen to the United States, but I now feel that we need to realize that there is no bodhisattva vow—no real effective wish to save all beings—outside of zazen, and no real zazen outside of the wish to save all beings. There's no compassion in addition to upright sitting, and no upright sitting in addition to compassion.

When Narasaki Roshi visited Tassajara, he talked about the three monkeys. I don't know the origin of these three monkeys; apparently, this teaching has been in Japan for a while. It's also familiar to us in the West. The way I heard the teaching of the three monkeys was, "See no evil, hear no evil, speak no evil." Is that the way you have heard it? Narasaki Roshi translated it as, "No seeing, no hearing, no speaking," or as, "No seeing evil, no hearing evil, no speaking evil," which means no seeing other people's faults, no speaking of other people's faults, and no listening to people who are talking about other people's faults. This is a regular Buddhist precept, isn't it?

On the deeper level of upright sitting itself, it's just plain "no seeing, no hearing, and no speaking."

Narasaki Roshi also said that nowadays everyone is quite eager to hear about other people's faults and speak about other people's faults, seeing if we can find out what's wrong with other people. Many people make a good living trying to find out what's wrong with the way people cook, the way people write, the way people make art, or the way people make movies. They find out what's wrong with them, tell everybody, and then everybody can tell everybody else. This is our way now, isn't it? Intense looking for, hearing about, and speaking about the faults of other people.

But Narasaki Roshi also said that we need a fourth monkey on top of these three, a fourth monkey of nonthinking. In other words, if we practice not seeing, not hearing, and not speaking evil with some fixed idea of what that means, this still can cause problems. In order to understand the precepts, we must practice nonthinking, *hishiryo*. If we engage in these three practices, and think about them and understand them only by our own thinking, we will have a tendency to say, "This is right and that is wrong. This is ethics. I am ethical; I am helping people." Therefore we need the fourth monkey, which protects us from self-righteousness by deeply reminding us that even the precepts are empty of inherent existence, that is, we understand them only in dynamic conversation with all living beings.

The fourth monkey is the nonabiding mind of upright sitting, the mind far beyond this world of virtue and nonvirtue. The precepts must be practiced with this mind of upright sitting in order to be received and lived, and not held to in some limited, fixed way. Receiving the precepts, we must practice upright sitting; we must practice nonthinking. The tricky part for Zen students is that in practicing nonthinking, sometimes we also forget about the precepts. If we don't receive and practice these precepts, the true meaning of nonthinking will not be transmitted to us. But if we don't practice nonthinking, the true meaning of these precepts will not be alive in us.

Zen Mind Temple
Tassajara Zen Mountain Center
Carmel Valley, California
Fall 1991

EIGHT

✵

Life Is Not Killed

What is it not to kill? When you meet a sentient being, to give complete attention to that sentient being, to be totally devoted to your friends, to your family, to your dog: that is not to kill, and that is what life is. If you practice like this, you will be instantly promoted from an ordinary human being into a buddha. Devotion is instant promotion. But it must be total. You can't be holding back even a little bit. Put your entire life into this being or this activity, without expecting anything. Stay close and do nothing, and you will instantly become a buddha, because that's what a buddha would do. That's what not to kill means.

Dogen says, "Life is not killed."[1] Not killing is not something you do, exactly, it's just the way things are, and your practice, then, is just the way things are. If you examine life thoroughly, you'll see that it's entirely interconnected. You cannot cut off an interconnected thing.

Life is not killed. This is a transcendent statement, not just a prohibitory one. A different translation of Dogen's commentary is, "One must not cut off life," and this matches our usual understanding of the precept. "Life is not killed" is very different from "One must not cut off life."

In the latter translation, Dogen Zenji is like a kindly grandmother, showing us a step-by-step practice by which we will become a buddha. But the way I'm reading the precept, it's not a step-by-step practice. It's a practice that's already over: buddha has already happened.

Bodhidharma says, "Self nature is subtle and mysterious. In the realm of everlasting dharma, not giving rise to the concept of killing is called the precept of not killing."

I think this means that when the mind does not believe in the concept of killing, life is not killed. And because life is not killed, the mind can rest completely in its nature, which is not to have a view of killing.

If life were killed, how could the mind rest? The mind is life. And in the mind at rest, life is not killed. A buddha's mind is so stupid that it can't think of such a clever thing as to cut off life. If a buddha could figure out how to do it, then a buddha could be a murderer. This is Bodhidharma's instruction. This is Dogen's instruction.

Kyogo, one of Dogen Zenji's direct disciples, wrote a commentary on what Dogen Zenji said about the precepts. "Living and dying are not before and after,"[2] he says. And the Buddhist precepts and Buddhist teachings, too, have nothing to do with before and after. We don't reject the world and say that there is no before and no after: human consciousness is involved in before and after. But there's another way, called Buddha's way, which is not about before and after.

Kyogo says, "Just not taking life is the manifestation of the whole works." This means that the whole, everything, is working. And "the whole works" also means the whole universe. Another translation of "the whole works" would be "total dynamic working." It's everything working with everything toward everything, all together. So life is the manifestation of the whole works. Death is the manifestation of the whole works. And just not taking life is the manifestation of the whole works.

When we understand that life is the manifestation of the whole works, the words *to kill* and *not to kill* are beyond their literal meanings. I think of the little wind bell hanging like a mouth in emptiness, not being concerned with north, south, east, west, good, or bad; just being a wind bell. Just hanging there as a manifestation of the whole works.

Life is just like this. Life is just living. Death is just dying. That's all. The wind bell is just hanging. The wind is just blowing. It moves the wind bell. The wind bell is just moving. It doesn't wish that it were moving in some other direction. It is manifesting its gravity and the movement of wind, and this is all that it does. It is the whole works and that's enough. And that's so simple that the human mind can't stand it. That's why we receive this precept again and again, so that we can stand being so simple.

Someone told me a story about this. This person was a monk at Tassajara, and a message was delivered to her that there was illness in the family. She has a good imagination, and she made up a world, a horrible world full of life that's not living and death that's not dying. She imagined a world of life that can be cut off, and dying happening to things. And she became very upset, right in the peaceful little valley of Tassajara. She tried to find out what was wrong, calling all over the world, eliminating some possibilities as she contacted certain relatives, but coming down to a more specific set of possibilities: something must have happened to one of her children.

Then she went to work in the kitchen, totally distraught. Even though she was in a Zen monastery, she was drowning in a poisonous sea. She was given a bunch of turnips to cut. She asked the turnips to save her—she appealed to each turnip as she took it in her hand—and the turnips saved her. She got to cut the turnips.

The world of before and after was always a hairsbreadth's deviation away, but by continuously going back to the turnip and cutting it—thump! thump! thump!—she was saved.

Later she found out that there had been a miscommunication, and everything that she had imagined was a dream. She was released from the bad dream, and now she imagined that all the people she loved were happy.

Then she realized that this was just a dream, too, and that the people she cared about might be utterly miserable. She couldn't know. But the point is that as she switched from dream to dream, where did her turnip go? She had lost her turnip again.

To go for refuge and to receive these precepts is like receiving a turnip. In fact, every moment we are given a turnip. And we just need to find out what is the turnip of this moment. What is the manifestation of the whole works right now? What frees us from this constant flow of dreams? What protects us from all the endless vanities?

Do you feel ready to be this sentient being? Do

you feel ready to receive the precept of completely being yourself? Buddha rejoices to see someone who receives this precept. Does anybody lack anything they need to receive this precept?

Suppose your back hurts. Suppose it feels as though a piece of heavy equipment were rolling over it. That's your turnip. A back with a steamroller going over it is a huge turnip. Be run over by it. That's what you have to work with. The way you get into the world beyond birth and death is through this body. This steamrollered body is your entrance into that other world.

Or maybe you have a lot of doubt. You don't believe that you can ever get to a world beyond birth and death. The not believing is another turnip that's given to you to save you. You have to have something to be saved by. Red, yellow, blue, green, white, form, not form, existing, not existing, cause and effect: we have to have something. You use the stuff of these dreams to save you from the dreams. In the midst of the dreams, you have to find something that you pick up and say, "This is my thing to work on."

But sometimes the pain is too much. Like the woman I just told you about, you go crazy. If the pain destroys your ability to practice patience, then you're cooked. You're temporarily disqualified from the game. But when you see the consequences of that, you come back. Maybe somebody walks up to you and says, "Sister, regain your presence of mind." Maybe the pain's not so bad anymore. Maybe it's the same. Maybe it's worse. But anyway, you come back into it, and you say, "I'm going to work with this turnip." Thump! "I'm going to receive the precept of life is not killed. I may have to cry my way into it. I may have to slide my way into it, but somehow I'm going to get into this body that I've got. I'm going to get into this mind that I've got. And I'm going to use this to save myself."

When human beings accept a precept, and they hear it in terms of past and future, they say, "Oh, I know what that means. I'll accept that precept." They are working on their ethics, which is fine. But when human beings accept a precept after hearing that this precept is not about past and future, then they have willingly accepted something that they do not understand. Usually people say, "I don't want anything that I don't understand. Get that away from me." They want to be able to say to themselves, I don't have any foreign bodies in here. Everything I've got here is part of my system. But when you know that these precepts are not in the realm of human comprehension, and you still receive them, you are like a buddha.

This receiving is free of marks. If someone gives you something that you don't understand, you just take it. You can just receive a turnip. Or in the morning, you can say to yourself, I receive this precept. It's a kind of ceremony. Life is not killed. You've not only received something that you don't understand, you've received something that is potent and vital.

This precept is about you being you completely. This, too, you do not understand. It is, after all, inexhaustibly vast to be you: you are the manifestation of the whole works.

After you receive the precept, you aren't different than you were before. But if you don't receive it, you don't know that. That's the advantage of receiving it. It's like wearing Buddha's robe. The point of putting on Buddha's robe is to understand that it doesn't make any difference. There's no difference between receiving the precept and not receiving it.

There are three levels on which to understand the precept not to kill. One level is the literal level, which is the same idea we grow up with in this culture: It's not right to kill. It's something that you *can* do but that you *must not* do. It's a given. In my childhood home, and yours, too, probably, killing was something we just didn't do.

The second level is the compassionate level. Sometimes you may need to kill in order to be helpful. Sometimes it's more compassionate to violate the precept in the literal sense, just as you need to lie sometimes in order to benefit beings.

At the third level, this precept is not talking about killing and not killing. This precept is pointing out that either of those ways of looking at things is violating Buddha's mind. Thinking that you can kill is violating this precept. Thinking you can keep this precept in a conventional sense is also violating this precept. If you are afraid of being killed, it's because you think that you can kill someone. People who believe that they can kill need some way to stop themselves from acting on their belief.

But to think of killing and to realize that it's not possible: that's not to think of killing. That's just seeing killing as a unicorn or a chocolate moon, a thought without substance. This precept points to the practice of living in this world without giving substance to the thought that you can kill.

Anybody who is afraid of being killed is somebody who thinks that he can kill somebody else. People go to war because they're afraid that they're going to be killed. But somebody who knows for sure that he can't kill anybody, somebody who knows for sure that he won't kill anybody, will not be afraid of being killed and therefore won't go to war. Not only that, but he won't be killed. And he won't die. Life doesn't die. Life is infinite and unbounded. Life is just living, and then it's gone. It changes. And if death happens, that's it. There's just death. Don't expect any other result.

If you let death be death, you go to heaven. But if you want death to give you some other result than death, that's misery, and you're not dying or going to heaven either. The other day, I heard someone say, "Everybody wants to go to heaven, but nobody wants to die." In order to go to heaven, you have to die. On time. Death's time, not yours. Also, you get to go to heaven if you just live, and for us human beings to be alive when we're alive, we have to die to before and after. And that's heaven: the same heaven as the heaven you go to when death is death.

You might ask, If life can't be killed, why would it matter if I stabbed a bunch of people? But why would you do that? Why would you stab people? Just to see the blood come out? A person who understands that life cannot be killed is a buddha. Why would a buddha want to stab somebody? A buddha looks at a person and sees a buddha. Why would a buddha stab a buddha? Such a being would absolutely not be able to kill anything.

According to worldly law, people do kill people. In the realm of ultimate truth, that doesn't happen, but Buddha can see that even the people who think according to worldly law are buddhas, too, and she sees that no matter what they think, their lives are not killed. Buddha can see that people act out a dream of killing one another. Buddha sees perfect beings causing themselves and one another misery, and Buddha does not see any life killed.

Buddhism doesn't contradict the conventional view of what happened, for example, during the Holocaust. Buddhism doesn't say, "That wasn't a problem." It *was* a problem. It *is* a problem. That's not what this precept is talking about.

Most of us have never seen anybody murdered. We've heard about it but we haven't seen it. In our own lives, perhaps the most horrific thing we've ever experienced is—*sesshin*. But in one way or another, we've experienced before-and-after mind. This precept is asking you to give up before-and-after mind and enter a different reality. It's saying that if you would die to before and after and enter the actual present moment, you could bring a light back to the world and teach people what it means not to kill.

Buddha understands the mind that thinks that we can be killed. Buddha doesn't say, "I don't know what you're talking about." Buddha comes into the world where people think that there's killing and not killing, and teaches. As a matter of fact, Buddha exists because of beings like that. Those beings evoke Buddha. If you have thoughts of before and after, and you believe in them, you're miserable, but if you have such thoughts and see that they're delusions, you're happy. In either case, Buddha sees buddha in you. Both views are perfect manifestations of the way things work.

Someone asked me if Buddha could go to San Quentin Prison and teach that life is not killed, and at the same time try to work against the death penalty. Buddha would go into the prison to teach people when the people in the prison were ready. If they were in the middle of a fight, Buddha wouldn't walk in there. And Buddha would go talk to the prison officials and the state government when they were ready to hear Buddha talk.

They're probably not going to say, "We're ready for Buddha to come talk to us." But when they're ready, they will express it in some way. If they're not ready, Buddha won't go and talk to them because it's a waste of time to talk to them before they're ready.

Everybody wants to know how to take care of things now before they die, or they want to know how they should take care of things after they die. "Before I go, what can I do?" Or "After I've died and given up my attachment to birth and death, and I've gone to Buddha's land, then what should I do?" But this precept is not talking about how to apply the precept. This precept is pointing to how to become a buddha. Once you're a buddha, you can talk to people about the details of how to apply it.

In order to practice this precept, you've got to expect no other result than just not to kill. "Not to kill is just not to kill. Not to kill is one precept; not to kill is ten precepts." Not to kill is the entire world. There's nothing else. There's no application. That's the precept.

Now, of course, if you accept the precept, you have just converted yourself into a beneficent being, and whatever you do will be beneficial in the world. And you can decide whether to stand outside of San Quentin, holding up a sign to abolish the death penalty. But you want everything you do to have some result right now. You don't want to be just who you are, just as you don't want to be totally devoted to another person, regardless of whether she improves her health, gets educated, gets better looking, likes you better, or gives you money: you don't want to do that. But that's what this precept is about. It's about total attention to this moment, to just sitting here, with no idea of any other result but just don't kill.

As Buddha said, you're like a person with an arrow in him who goes to the doctor and says, "What extraction procedure are you going to use? Is there going to be an infection following this? Am I going to be as good as I was before? Am I going to be as good looking, or better looking?"

After you believe that not to kill is just not to kill, do you think you could go stab people? And their blood wouldn't matter? Of course not. But when you receive the precept, you're giving up control, and you don't know what you're going to do after that. You can't go into Buddha's realm saying, "Well, I'll go in there, but you've got to guarantee that I won't do anything wrong after this, that I'll be politically correct afterward, that people will still like me." In fact, you will be more compassionate than you are now, more effective than you are now, but maybe not in the same way.

We have to give up everything to enter Buddha's realm, but we don't have to kill ourselves. We just have to stay in the present, which is exactly the same as dying to each moment so we can be alive in each moment. It's not a violent thing. You've got to do it kindly. You have to be patient with yourself, and notice how difficult it is to let go of this conceptual mind and enter a realm where you can just suffer.

I don't mean to say it's easy to give up everything. I know it's hard. In the meantime, please try to acknowledge your suffering and sit patiently in the middle of it, with all sentient beings. When we sit patiently in the presence of our pain, we can see the outlines of birth and death, and we can see our attachments. And then we can see where to let go.

Zen Mind Temple
Tassajara Zen Mountain Center
Carmel Valley, California
February 7, 1992

NINE

❖

The Home Altar

The home altar for a Zen student is right here. The way comes forth from here and it returns here. This is the altar of nondual meditation, the altar that is not an object of thought.

When Dogen Zenji's teacher, Tientung Rujing, was being installed as abbot in a monastery, he walked into the hall, looked at the buddha on the altar, and said, "A poison dart in my eye." Then he walked on. Zen is iconoclastic: we rebel against any icons that are outside ourselves. An altar is a place where we express our nondual relationship with our true nature, not a place to make offerings to a buddha that is other than ourselves, or to an awakening that is somewhere else.

If you want to set up an altar in your house, look for a place that feels good to you—a "home within your home." Don't put it in a place where it might disturb other members of your household or visitors. Start with a place for yourself, a place that you can feel refreshed by.

When you set up an altar, it's good to have a central image. You could, like the early Buddhists, use a wheel, a foot-print, or a stone pillar; it could be a statue or picture of a buddha, a being who personifies enlightenment; or it could be a statue or picture of an enlightening being, such as Avalokitesvara, the Bodhisattva of Infinite Compassion, who hears the cries of all beings. You could even write on a card the name of a buddha or bodhisattva—"Avalokitesvara" or "Hearer of the Cries of the World"—and put that card in the center of the altar.

The buddha or bodhisattva goes in the middle. To its left, put a candle, and to its right, a flower. Light is considered the highest of the physical offerings. The light of the candle, the smell of the flower, and in the middle, right in front of the figure, put an incense bowl. Any bowl, ceramic or metal, would be suitable. You could fill it with sand, but ash from the fireplace works best, and as you use it, ash from the incense you offer will gradually build up.

In addition to offering light, flowers, and incense, offer teachings that you chant yourself. You could chant scriptures or something that you feel is dharma, truly awakened teaching. Offer it before the statue to bring the joy of the teaching to Buddha and to yourself.

Many of us Westerners entered Zen through sitting meditation, and we were shocked to see that traditional Zen practice involves ritual activities such as bowing. I heard about a German woman who was studying Zen in Japan. Once during a ceremony, as she was bowing, she said to someone nearby, "*I don't know what I'm doing down here, but the rest of me does.*" When bowing, you go down to the earth; you touch the earth with your feet, your knees, your hands, and your head. Bowing is Buddhism: where there's bowing, there's Buddhism, and when there's Buddhism, there's bowing. To bow is not to bow down to something. To bow is actually to crack duality. The longer I study Zen, the more I realize how deeply devotional it is.

There really isn't any buddha outside yourself. Putting buddhas on altars, and also taking buddhas off altars, is a way to encounter this most vital issue. You need some way to encounter it. I think it's really an auspicious opportunity when you put a buddha on an altar in your house: this way you can somehow deal with the issue of your buddhahood. The altar is a place you can use to return home and celebrate the intimacy of all living beings with the awakened ones. It's a place you can use to express the tender feeling of being Buddha's child as well as the bold feeling of being Buddhism.

Zen Mind Temple
Tassajara Zen Mountain Center
Carmel Valley, California
Spring 1987

TEN

❂

Just This Person

I want to say a few words to encourage all of us to practice upright sitting. My intention to speak in this way comes from my faith and understanding that upright sitting is the way of entering the self-fulfilling awareness that all the awakened ancestors of our tradition have held to be the true path of peace and freedom for all living beings.

For me, upright sitting means you are thoroughly and completely yoursef, so that by fully acknowledging and expressing your limited individuality, you totally transcend it. By sitting still in each moment of your life and becoming just yourself, you may finally realize that you are not yourself at all, but that in reality you are so deeply connected with others and so completely supported by others that, in fact, you are nothing other than all living beings. Realizing this is realizing Buddha's mind because Buddha's mind is the mind of all sentient beings. In such a way, you are awakened from your fundamental human delusion that you are separate from others, and thus you are free from all the misery that is born of this delusion.

Just before leaving his teacher, Good Servant (Dongshan Liangjie) asked him, "If after one hundred years, someone should ask if I am able to portray the master's truth, how should I respond?"

Cloudy Cliff (Yunyan Tansheng) paused for a while and then said, "Just this person."

Good Servant was lost in thought. Cloudy Cliff said, "Good Servant, having assumed the burden of this great matter, you must be very cautious."

Good Servant remained dubious about what Cloudy Cliff had said. Later, as he was crossing a river, he saw his own reflection and experienced a great awakening to the meaning of the previous exchange. He composed the following *gatha:*

Earnestly avoid seeking outside,

Or it will recede far from your self.

Now I walk alone,

Yet everywhere I meet him.

He is no other than myself,

But I am not he.

Only by understanding in this way

Will you directly merge with suchness.[1]

When I wholeheartedly practice the teaching of "just this person," all beings come forth to meet me, and I realize that they are now no other than myself, no matter what their form in terms of race, gender, species, and so on.

The way of freedom from self-delusion comes forth from the thorough acknowledgment of such delusion. Our compassionate ancestors studied, understood, and taught completely how self-delusion arises and how it is the source of all our misery. Buddhas are those who deeply enter into learning about self-delusion and are greatly awakened in the midst of studying self-delusion.

We call the gate to this liberating study of the self upright sitting.

Our great ancestor Henry David Thoreau writes in *Walden*, "You only need sit still long enough in some attractive spot in the woods that all its inhabitants may exhibit themselves to you by turns."[2]

By sitting still, you enter into the real study of the self. By just sitting, you give up mediating your experience, or preparing yourself for it. Thus the self that comes to you through upright sitting is not the self you choose to study and not the self you expect to study, but the self that "may exhibit [itself] to you by turns" when you just sit. It is a fresh, unexpected, troublesome, difficult, immediate self. This is the self that's fruitful to study, because when the self that appears is fresh and immediate and not what you expect, you are shocked out of your numb complacency and into total engagement with it.

I find that the more troubled I am by an event, the more immediate it is; and the more immediate, the more engaging. So I'm interested in what's fresh and immediate for people, and lately, as a way of finding what's most immediate I've been asking people, "What is bothering you most?" One person answered that she has been bothered by her swallowing while she is sitting in the zendo. It's not that she couldn't swallow, but rather that she was doing it often and noisily. She was troubled and worried that her swallowing might be bothering her neighbors. As she continued to sit and watch her breathing and swallowing and worrying, she noticed something else. She noticed that the reason she was worried about bothering others was that she was afraid they would dislike her for the noises she was making. She was bothered by a fear that she would be disliked. After telling me about all this, she said, "Is this kind of the right direction?"

I was very happy to hear her story of upright sitting and said, "I don't think it's right or wrong, but I do think it's very good that through your sitting you are becoming more engaged with yourself." This self was not the self she might have chosen to study, but an unexpected self that she witnessed being born in the experience of swallowing, worrying, and fear.

At first, she thought she was concerned about bothering or harming others, but sitting and looking more deeply, things turned around, and she saw that she was worried about others harming her. She first thought that she was concerned about others, but she came to realize that she was really concerned about herself.

In our tradition, there are innumerable stories like this that show that when you sincerely practice the ancestor's simple instruction of "just this person," you will see how completely contradictory an independent self is, and the more you see how self-contradictory the self is, the more you will realize who you really are and the more you will be fulfilled. The more fully you can affirm the contradictory nature of your self, the more fully you can affirm the contradictions in your life. And if you can fully affirm these contradictions, you will be able to affirm your death. Thus you will have the courage to just sit and be your self beyond your idea of your self—your self in complete identity with what it is not—namely, all living beings. This process culminates in your realizing that you are completely identical with the other, thus freeing you from your basic delusion of a separate self.

Here is one more story of sitting upright. When George Washington Carver was a little boy, he lived in the foothills of the Ozark Mountains in Missouri. On a piece of remote and unused land, he created his own little garden. From discarded material, he built a secret greenhouse far back in the woods. When asked what he was doing out in the woods, he said, "I go to my garden hospital and take care of many sick plants." He took sick plants to his greenhouse and nursed them until they became well; they became healthy. He knew how to heal the plants. The women in his neighborhood heard about him and asked if he would take care of their sick houseplants. He did. He took care of them, and then he returned them when they were healthy again. They asked him, "How do you know how, where did you learn how, to heal these plants?" And George said, "All the flowers talk to me, and so do the hundreds of other living things. I learn what I know by watching and loving everything."

"Watching and loving everything" was his way of upright sitting. This was his gate into the true study of self. He realized himself through his intimacy with the plants, through his listening to the flowers. Watching and loving them was his fulfillment. For him, the plants were not something external. They were the flowering of his genius, and by fulfilling him they were healed.

Sitting upright with innumerable living things, we naturally enter the self-fulfilling awareness of buddha, the awareness that liberates and heals all living beings.

Green Dragon Temple
Green Gulch Farm
Sausalito, California
Summer 1993

ELEVEN

✸

Longing for Oneness

The mountains and rivers of the immediate present
are the manifestation of the path of the ancient buddhas.
Because they are the self before the emergence of signs, they
are the penetrating liberation of ultimate reality.

Master Daokai said, "Green mountains are forever
walking. A stone woman bears a child by night."

If one knows one's own walking, one knows the
walking of the green mountains. There should be an
examination of both stepping back and stepping forward.

–Eihei Dogen, Mountains and Rivers Sutra

I've been told—but I don't
know for sure—that you're like me. If I could speak for
you, I would say that you have a deep longing for oneness,
a deep urge to return to your original face before your
parents were born.

The sutra just quoted talks about "the mountains
and rivers of the immediate present." How can you return
to the immediate present? These mountains of the immediate present are the self before the emergence of subtle
signs. Your existence in the immediate present is the self
before the emergence of signs.

When we try to chant "The Merging of Difference
and Oneness" during morning service, sometimes there are

great differences in the pitch of our voices. When we feel the painful difference, we yearn for oneness. Some of us, in trying to make the oneness happen, just make more difference. It's so discouraging to try to make difference turn into oneness: you can't do it. Difference is difference and oneness is oneness. But in the mountains and rivers of the immediate present, difference and oneness are merged.

Anything we dream of is something we want to be reunited with. Everything we see, we hear, and we touch is what we want to be reunited with. Everything we experience we are separated from. Turning around, stepping back: this is practice. Once we step back, we naturally step forward. But before we step back, we don't know what to do. We're not settled, we're not satisfied. When we step back from the world, we step back from where we are, and if we have any reservations at all about where we are, we cannot step back. When you and I are willing to be right here, right now, wholeheartedly, we can step back. We can turn around.

I'm expressing an aching heart. My heart is like water trying to return to the ocean. If I can simply accept this, it's enough. "What does this pain ask of me?" "What does this person ask of me?" "What does this bird ask of me?" An answer may come. The answer may be, "Turn it around." Or "Let go." Or "Come home." Or "Scratch my back." You may get an answer; that's okay. But don't stop questioning. "What does this ask of me?" is simply a way to talk about unambivalent presence. It's a construction to help you let go of constructions. But it is not really a way back: you're already there.

You may think I'm explaining something to you, but I'm just expressing myself. Hearts are meant to bleed: that's what they're built for.

There are about eighty people in this *sesshin*, and we are all packed into one room, so, unfortunately, some of the seats are not so good. Some of the people who got bad seats were moved to other bad seats. They are currently in some new bad seats, due to the compassion of the practice leaders. Our bleeding hearts sense your difficulty and we want to make you more comfortable. We don't mean to inflict pain on you by putting you behind posts two inches from the wall, next to people you don't like. We don't mean to. But in our own stupid way we may be being very kind to you, giving you a chance to practice grateful mind. You are in a situation, a painful situation, where things are quite different from what you expected. Many people are experiencing emotional pain—almost stronger than the physical pain they are experiencing in their legs—regarding their seating assignment. One older student actually almost ran out of the zendo because of her seating assignment. Just as she tried to flee, the supernatural powers of the practice leaders moved her to a different seat. She's sitting very still now in her good seat. Some other people didn't get their seats changed, and they were even luckier, because their terrible situation turned around. How did they do it? How did they go from "This is impossible" to "Oh, I'm so grateful"? How did it happen? It happened.

Seating assignments are wonderful opportunities to turn it around, relatively easy compared with personal relationships with other beings. Our bleeding hearts want to turn it around with each other; we want to be reunited with each other, but we need the other person to help; somehow we can't just unite on our own. Because the other person can wink, we wait for them. We say, "I can't believe that you love me unless you wink at me. Please wink. I can't believe you feel my heart reaching for you until you reach back. I can't believe you trust my outstretched hand unless you take it."

These are instructions in practice. We find these instructions in many places. As Shakespeare says in *Hamlet*,

> *Horatio.* Oh, day and night, but this is
> wondrous strange!
>
> *Hamlet.* And therefore as a stranger give it
> welcome.
> There are more things in heaven
> and earth, Horatio,
> Than are dreamt of in your philosophy.[1]

And we yearn for oneness. How can I express my yearning? With my mouth I express my yearning; with my body I ask the question, What? What is it? What is birth and death? What does it ask of me? What is it that cares?

Green Dragon Temple
Green Gulch Farm
Sausalito, California
Spring 1985

TWELVE

❂

Cooking in the Cauldron of All Beings

Almost exactly half my life has been lived in Zen temples and monasteries. In the morning, I rise before dawn and shuffle sleepily to the zendo. Though painful difficulties often arise, friends and teachers are extremely kind and helpful to me. I cannot find words to fully express my gratitude and sense of good fortune for such a life. Trying to live a life of awakening is a joy beyond joy. Now it is autumn and I am approaching fifty. All around me and inside me, there is dying and sadness. I deeply question what real compassion is. How may I live the rest of my life to repay the love and kindness I have been given and to fulfill my responsibility for the welfare of all suffering beings? How can something helpful come from these mixed feelings?

Up until now, I have practiced by sitting still in the midst of all living beings, that is, by walking straight ahead in the buddha way. Yet I sense that something is missing, and, at times, I hear the echo of a voice saying, Reach out. In the past few years, I feel a change in my practice. I wonder, is reaching out something different from the way I am already living, or is it just doing what I am already doing more thoroughly and carefully?

Perhaps reaching out will naturally develop from wholehearted devotion to the small tasks that appear before me every day. Perhaps caring for the near will somehow accomplish the far-reaching work of compassion. Yet I can't help feeling uneasy with this devotion to the small and the near unless I hold the thought of universal compassion in my heart and in my mind. In fact, I can't even really take care of the small things in my life without the support of others. Or, turning it around, only by devotion to the well-being of others am I able to accomplish the smallest things.

The authentic practice of sitting still in the depths of silence and coming to understand Buddha's teaching is not accomplished by yourself. The true significance of Buddha's radical instruction "Just sit" cannot be realized except in the context of the vow to save all living beings.

In the midst of such thoughts and feelings, I find comfort and encouragement in the stories of our ancestral founders. Please consider this anecdote.

The monk Daokai went to study with Master Touzi. He asked, "The sayings of the buddhas and founders are like everyday rice and tea. Do they have anything else to help people?"

Touzi said, "You tell me: Do the emperor's commands in his own realm depend on the ancient kings?"

As Daokai was about to speak, Touzi hit him with his whisk and said, "The moment you intended to come here, you already deserved a beating." At this Daokai was awakened.[1]

It warms my heart to find my question reflected in Daokai's question: Did the buddhas and founders teach anything other than this everyday activity? Does repaying kindness and benefiting beings depend on anything outside of meticulous attention to moment-by-moment experience? Does our everyday practice of compassion depend on the authority of the ancient buddhas? The response to this question is contained in the rest of the story.

There are two approaches to settling your body-mind into the buddha way. The first is going to a teacher and listening to the teaching; the second is total devotion to just sitting. Listening to the teaching opens your heart-mind and allows it to work freely. Just sitting is the everyday affair of the buddhas and the living realization of the Zen founders. Neither approach can be neglected.

The story indicates that first you go in faith to receive help from another. And then, in accepting this help, you find it in yourself. First the truth turns you, and then you turn the truth.

Recently, I went to an art show, a presentation of life-size dolls. The woman who made them also teaches doll making. She said that doll making is a way for people to manifest their deepest affirmation in form. Listening to her, I thought of the way of just sitting: manifesting in the sitting posture your deepest affirmation, clarifying the body-mind, and awakening to reality. In the buddhadharma, the true reality is free of form and formlessness, but it must be brought into form in order to be healing.

The doll maker also explained that these dolls are always created within a circle of friends. What is a circle? A circle is a two-dimensional image. In three dimensions, we might call it a cauldron, a crucible, or a womb container for the process in which the highest aspiration of your life comes into form.

So the circle is a relationship: a relationship of mutual commitment and support. It can be created by just two people. A student and teacher working together, discussing the dharma form, the container in which they realize the total devotion to just sitting. Knowing that the process cannot be realized by an individual alone, each person in the circle seeks and gives help, thus strengthening the cauldron and allowing the contents to be cooked to perfection. Teachers and friends need us to realize our truest and most perfect potential, and they won't be happy until we accomplish this.

Practicing in the cauldron with friends and teachers may protect us from clinging to limited ideas of what sitting practice is. For example, in the process of realizing the buddha way through our sitting, we are likely to develop a narrow attitude about what awakening is. We may think that we have it or that we don't have it.

Entering the meditation hall and sitting in the midst of friends and teachers may actually be seen as a request for guidance. We sit down and thus ask for guidance from everyone. "This is my practice: this is my offering to all beings. This is my attempt to manifest in form my highest aspiration. What do you think, folks?" Guidance may be received when a teacher walks around the meditation hall adjusting posture.

Sometimes you may feel that you are sitting quite

straight, and after being adjusted you may feel crooked. It's not that you were right or wrong, but rather that you now have new information about what you are. Someone has touched you and through this touch has said, I love you and really want you to be completely happy. And, by the way, please try this posture. How does this feel? And if you still don't feel that you are receiving guidance, you need to say out loud to our teacher, "How is my practice, what is the truth?" By asking, you create the cauldron and you stir the soup.

Each of you—not separately, but in the cauldron with all beings, cooking and being cooked—is realizing awakening. Not you by yourself, because that is not who you really are. You by yourself are not buddha nature; but your total being in the cauldron of all beings is realizing the buddha way. This is the total exertion of your life.

You also can't really be flexible and free of fixed views by yourself. To decide for yourself what flexibility is is a kind of rigidity. Living in harmony with all beings is flexibility. It is a kind of cosmic democracy. Each of us has a role in the situation and gets one vote. You cast your vote by being here like a great unmoving mountain. Please cast your vote completely: that is your job. Then listen to all other beings, especially foreigners, especially strangers, and especially enemies.

Hang out with people who are capable of making a commitment to you and your life, and who require that you make a commitment to theirs. Hang out with people who care about you, with people who need you to develop and who say so. Make such a commitment and don't break that bond until you and all beings are perfect.

You can't make the buddha-body without a cauldron, and you can't make a cauldron by yourself. You can't practice all by yourself: that is delusion. Everything coming forward and confirming you is awakening. Then you are really cooking.

Green Dragon Temple
Green Gulch Farm
Muir Beach, California
Fall 1988

PART THREE

⚙

TIME AND SEASON

Song of the Jewel
Mirror Samadhi

The teaching of thusness has been intimately
communicated by buddhas and ancestors;
Now you have it, so keep it well.
Filling a silver bowl with snow, hiding a heron in the
moonlight—
When you array them, they're not the same,
When you mix them, you know where they are.
The meaning is not in the words,
Yet it responds to the arrival of energy.
If you're excited, it becomes a pitfall;
If you miss it, you fall into retrospective hesitation.
Turning away and touching are both wrong.
For it is like a mass of fire.
Just to depict it in literary form is to relegate it
to defilement.
It is bright just at midnight; it doesn't appear at dawn.
It acts as a guide for beings; its use removes all pains.
Although it is not fabricated, it is not without speech.
It is like facing a jewel mirror;
Form and image behold each other—
You are not it; it actually is you.

It is like a babe in the world, in five aspects complete;

It does not go or come, nor rise nor stand.

Baba wawa—is there anything said or not?

Ultimately it does not apprehend anything,

Because its speech is not yet correct.

It is like the six lines of the double split hexagram;

The relative and absolute integrate;

Piled up, they make three;

The complete transformation makes five.

It is like the taste of the five flavored herb,

Like the diamond thunderbolt.

Subtly included within the true,

Inquiry and response come up together.

Communing with the source and communing

with the process,

It includes integration and includes the road;

Merging is auspicious; do not violate it.

Naturally real yet inconceivable,

It is not within the province of delusion

or enlightenment.

With causal conditions, time and season,

Quiescently it shines bright.

In its fineness it fits into spacelessness;

In its greatness it is utterly beyond location.

A hairsbreadth's deviation will fail to accord

with the proper attunement.

Now there are sudden and gradual,

In connection with which are set up basic approaches.

Once basic approaches are distinguished,

then there are guiding rules.

But even though the basis is reached

and the approach comprehended,

True eternity still flows.

Outwardly still while inwardly moving,

Like a tethered colt, a trapped rat;

The ancient saints pitied them,

and bestowed upon them the teaching;

According to their delusions, they called black as white.

When erroneous imaginations cease,

the acquiescent mind realizes itself.

If you want to conform to the ancient way,

Please observe the ancients of former times.

When about to fulfill the way of buddhahood,

one gazed at a tree for ten eons,

Like a tiger leaving part of its prey,

a horse with a white left hind leg.

Because there is the base, there are jewel pedestals,

fine clothing.

Because there is the startlingly different,

there are house cat and cow.

Yi, with his archer's skill, could hit a target

at a hundred paces.

But when arrow points meet head on,

what has this to do with the power of skill?

When the wooden man begins to sing,

the stone woman gets up to dance.

It's not within reach of feeling or discrimination,

How could it admit of consideration in thought?

A minister serves the lord, a son obeys the father.
Not obeying is not filial, and not serving is no help.
Practice secretly, working within, as though a fool,
like an idiot.
If you can achieve continuity, this is called the host
within the host.

THIRTEEN

✸

Warm Smiles from Cold Mountains

Sesshin can be seen as a week in which you will sit and deepen your practice, and perhaps recognize something of the nature of mind. This is one traditional approach. It is the gate of cultivation, entering enlightenment from ordinariness. Another way to see it is that for seven days you are maintaining the essential working of the buddha way. It's not so much that you do a week's sitting in order to get somewhere or see something, but you do a week's sitting in order to do a week's sitting. You do one week of Buddha's work; you do one week of Buddha's play. This is the natural gate, entering ordinariness from enlightenment.

"The Song of the Jewel Mirror Samadhi" starts, "The teaching of thusness has been intimately communicated by buddhas and ancestors; / Now you have it, so keep it well." The starting point is buddhahood. "Now you have it." The rest of the poem explains how to keep it well. How do you keep it well? By doing Buddha's work. So if you see your practice this way, then just take it easy. Relax and enjoy yourself. This is not a technique to accomplish anything: it is simply the daily activity of Buddha.

It is said that when asked what he learned in China, the young master Dogen said, "The eyes are horizontal, the nose vertical. I came back empty-handed. So now I just while away my time and take things as they come."

Most buddhas have open, empty hands. If you're a buddha, you don't need to have something in your hand. You are the attainment: you are the practice. You don't need any extra equipment. A nice thing about *sesshin* is that it's so simple. All you have to do is sit and that's enough. You can enjoy yourself. Enjoy the simple fact that your eyes are horizontal and your nose is vertical. Mark time, just take things as they come. Just take this breath as it comes, this breath as it goes, this sitting posture, this sound of the stream. This is what our ancestor Dogen Zenji called the "self-enjoyment samadhi" *(jijuyu zammai)*.

After Buddha was awakened, he sat and enjoyed the bliss of freedom *(vimoksha-sukha-samadhi)* under the bodhi tree for seven days. Can we give ourselves permission to simply sit and enjoy the bliss of liberation? Will I give myself that permission? Will you give yourself that permission? I encourage you to enjoy yourself as Buddha's work.

Could it be that to enjoy yourself as you sit is Buddha's work? Do you have any doubt about that? If you have doubt about it, it is Buddha's work to enjoy that doubt. Examine that doubt. See if that doubt has any substance.

I don't say we shouldn't desire to accomplish something. I say, let's encourage ourselves to become free of our impulse to accomplish something. Let's live in the midst of desires for attainment and improvement without being ensnared by them and see that as Buddha's work, understand that as Buddha's work. This is to settle into the samadhi of self-enjoyment. Our ancestors say it's not that there's no attainment: buddhas have great attainment. It's just that their practice in realization and their realization in practice is undefiled, unstained by attainment.

The Tathagata's body cannot be seen by marks. This doesn't mean it doesn't have any marks, but you can't recognize it by marks. As the Diamond Sutra says, the Tathagata's body is "marked by no-marks." The famous Japanese folk potter Shoji Hamada didn't sign his bowls. People asked him, "Why don't you sign them?" He responded in jest, saying, "Well, if people find unsigned bowls that are no good, they won't blame me for them, and if they see unsigned bowls that are good, they'll say they are mine." Similarly, the Tathagata is unmarked, unsigned.

Arhats are marked. So if you look at Buddhist statues, arhats are sometimes depicted as deformed and ugly. This means that their bodies are marked by their great attainments. But bodhisattvas are not deformed, because there is no sign of attainment. That doesn't mean that there isn't any attainment, but that there's no sign of attainment. Don't deface yourself by attainment. Don't sprout some accomplishment on your unmarked buddha-body. Well, I shouldn't say don't do it. Go ahead: do it if you want to. But already you are doing Buddha's work. You are maintaining the buddha way in the world.

The teaching of thusness is not captured in words, and yet it is spoken. However, as "The Song of the Jewel Mirror Samadhi" says, "Just to depict it in literary form is to relegate it to defilement." Still, it is okay to defile it: it is okay to speak about it. As the great teacher Zhaozhou says, "It knowingly and deliberately transgresses."

At this time of year, it's cold at Tassajara. Ed Brown and I were reminiscing about the old days at Tassajara, when some of the students made vows to attain all kinds of things. A vow that was made during one of the first practice periods was to go through the whole practice period wearing nothing more than a tee shirt under a thin gray robe. Two or three people made that vow. It was quite cold that practice period, and one of the people who made this vow sat by the door of the unheated zendo. He made it through the first few days of the December *sesshin*. Then he went into his room, got into his sleeping bag, and didn't come out for the rest of the *sesshin*.

During that time, some of us in the practice period sent a greeting to Richard Baker, in Japan. I said, "Warm smiles from cold mountains."

So here we are, warm smiles in the cold mountains. We're still here, eighteen years later. We still have warm smiles, warm bodies, and warm hearts in these cold mountains. The interpenetration of warm bodies and cold mountains is also form and emptiness. You can't separate warm bodies and cold mountains. As long as you're alive, you've got both going on. When you're in your sleeping bag, maybe you can separate warm bodies and cold mountains for a little while. Then you've got just warm bodies and warm sleeping bags, which is okay. But walking around at Tassajara, the dynamic interpenetration of form and emptiness is demonstrated.

I don't like the cold, but I love the cold. When I walk in the cold wind, I hate it, but I feel myself surrounded by the truth. I feel I am in the right place. The cold wind is so invigorating, so vital. And I hate it. I feel both of those things. I'm afraid the cold will take away my warm smile and warm heart. Certainly it can take away my warm fingers and warm toes. Can I find a way for this warm person to be settled in the cold mountains? If I stay too warm, I'll be afraid of the cold. If I get too cold, I'll be afraid of the cold. What is Buddha's work in the middle of the cold? Have a dialogue with the cold, a dialogue with emptiness. Stare at the cold, stare at the not-you. If you look at it long enough, it will look back at you. The cold mountains will smile.

The Tang dynasty poet Cold Mountain (Han-Shan) said this:

> [People] these days search for a way
> through the clouds,
> But the cloud way is dark and without sign.
> The mountains are high and often steep
> and rocky;
> In the broadest valleys the sun seldom shines.
> Green crests before you and behind,
> White clouds to east and west—
> Do you want to know where the cloud way lies?
> There it is, in the midst of the Void![1]

This poem is well suited for Tassajara. "In the broadest valleys the sun seldom shines"—not to mention the narrow valleys, such as this one. If you walk up the road, the sun is shining, but down here it's not. Green crests are ahead of you and behind you, and white clouds are to the east and the west.

You are maintaining the essential working of the buddha way. But there is some danger of slipping on the steep mountains of attainment. There is some tendency to try to do a higher-quality job of maintaining the buddha way. So all the teaching is intended, first of all, to empower you to carry out Buddha's work, and then to protect you from thinking that you have to add something to that. I encourage you to do the practice that you're already doing. You don't need to add anything else.

The lineage of Soto Zen, particularly as it comes down through Suzuki Roshi, is a lineage of cloud drivers and cloud farmers. It is the way of the clouds, and the way through the clouds. It may sometimes seem difficult because it can't be recognized by marks. It is unmarked. Unmarked means it is you. Unmarked means you're Buddha. This is the face that you have, so enjoy yourself and continue your work.

Zen Mind Temple
Tassajara Zen Mountain Center
Carmel Valley, California
Fall 1985

FOURTEEN

✺

Suchness

During morning service, we chant from "The Song of the Jewel Mirror Samadhi": "The teaching of thusness has been intimately communicated by buddhas and ancestors; / Now you have it, so keep it well."

The first point I would like to make about this teaching is this: If you want to practice suchness, you should do so without delay. That's the way that suchness is always practiced: without delay. In other words, *right now*. Not later, when you're better prepared: that's not the practice of suchness. There are practices that you can prepare for, but I want to talk about the practice that is done without delay.

What is it that I can do without delay? Well, actually, there's nothing that I can do without delay. But everything is being done without delay. I can't do anything without delay, because as soon as I try to do something without delay, I am delaying. "I" am in the way, causing a delay.

Things are constantly happening without delay. Everything is on time. "Everything being on time" is the practice of suchness. Not that I make things be on time, but that things are on time: that's me. I am just everything happening without delay. The practice of suchness is not something that I do or you do. Right now, it is happening: you have that practice right now. You already have it, so please take care of it.

This same thread runs through all Buddhist practices, this nondelay practice. It is a practice that is not done by anyone, and it is a practice that confirms everyone. It's not that people confirm the practice, but rather that the practice confirms people. In addition, everyone is completely confirmed, not just a little bit confirmed. Each person, on her own individual path, with whatever unique characteristics or habits she has, is confirmed by the nondelay of all things.

There is a story about two of our Chinese ancestors, men I wish I could have met. They lived a long time ago, around 1500 years back. One was named Nanyue Huairang, and the other was named Dajen Huineng. Huineng is sometimes called the sixth ancestor of Zen. Nearly all the living schools of Zen Buddhism trace their lineages to him and come from his heart. One of his most illustrious disciples was Nanyue Huairang.

When Huairang came to Huineng to study, Huineng said, "Where do you come from?"

Huairang replied, "I come from Sungshan."

Huineng then said, "What is this that thus comes?"

To which Huairang answered, "As soon as I say it's this, I already miss the point completely."

The great master Huineng said, "Well then, is there no practice and realization?"

Huairang calmly replied, "I don't say there's no practice and realization, just that it cannot be defiled."

The great master was very happy to hear this and he said, "All buddhas practice this non-defiling way. You are thus. I am thus too."[1]

The practice cannot be defiled. In other words, it cannot be delayed. It's always marching ahead, unhindered, and completely happy. There's nothing we can do about it—nothing we can do, even if we try, to interfere with the great way. For example, if I try to be a better person, I'm already defiling myself. I have no ability to "improve" myself, not by "me" trying to. "I" don't even know what "improvement" is. Yet this doesn't mean that it is impossible to change, that there's no practice and no realization. The point is that if I jump into the act and try to cause practice and realization, I defile them. I say, "This is such-and-so," and I miss it completely. Transformation is not something that I can do: transformation does me.

As I said before, this practice is very difficult to do properly. It's hard to get out of the way and let it happen. Because we have trouble doing this practice, buddhas sometimes lend us a hand, provide a way. But remember, there are no ways to do this. There's nothing you can use to help you practice suchness. There's no way you can get a lever on it. All the same, buddhas provide levers and methods because some people refuse to try unless they're given some way to try. As I said, "You already have it"— but you may not believe it.

There is an expression that describes two aspects of the practice of suchness: "the grasping way and the granting way." "You already have it" is the grasping way. And honoring the doubt that "you already have it" is the granting way.

Emperor Wu asked Bodhidharma, "What is the highest meaning of the holy truths?"

Bodhidharma replied, "Vast emptiness and no holiness."[2]

Holiness is something extra, something added on to things as they are. For Buddha, there is no such thing as "holiness," nothing on top of things as they are.

After Bodhidharma's exchange with Emperor Wu, he went away and sat for nine years, facing a wall. That was just the way it was. Very few people of his time could appreciate him, so he didn't have many disciples. It was hard to practice that way. It was so simple and, besides, he was kind of unfriendly looking, just sitting there like a wall.

Now we may be able to see how this unfriendly-looking guy was pure compassion. He was unfriendly to anything but suchness. The greatest compliment he could offer to all sentient beings was simply suchness. He didn't tell anybody anything that they could do to improve themselves. Instead, he said, "You already have it." Uncompromising, unswerving steadfastness in suchness. This is the grasping way.

Once upon a time, a Zen teacher came to our mountain monastery at Tassajara, and he said that in monastic life, it's as if someone puts a giant hand around the monastery and squeezes the monastery. Squeezes each person right down onto herself. Squeezes the people into the schedule, into their seats, into their lunches. And squeezes tighter and tighter until somebody pops out. When somebody pops out, you scoop her up and put her right back in, and squeeze again, until the next person pops out. We don't know whom it will be: it could be a new student, it could be the abbot. Then you scoop him up and pop him back in and squeeze. You squeeze yourself into the practice of suchness. If anyone can't stand it, well, scoop him up in terms of whatever he can do, and put him back inside.

Scooping people up and putting them back inside is the granting way. That is, if they refuse to believe that they already have received the teaching of suchness, you say, "Okay, you're right, you can't do suchness. So do this practice that I outline for you, which you *can* do." Secretly, they are scooped up and put back into the practice of suchness.

Although you may not like it, the first principle of Buddhism is Buddha's mind. I say you may not like it because what is Buddha's mind? You already have it and you may wish that Buddha's mind were something different from what you have. However, the first principle is that our minds and Buddha's mind are the same.

The second principle is that we think that our minds and Buddha's mind are different. This principle concerns inequality, concerns differences. Because we live in the day-to-day world of differences, it's hard for us to appreciate the first principle: the equality of ourselves and the buddhas. We make differences, we manufacture inequalities, so we perceive them everywhere. These two principles have to be lived with, and these two together are suchness. Even in our differences, we always practice without delay, even though we say, "Delay. Wait." Saying, "Delay" always happens on time.

For living beings, to be awake is simply not to move. We cannot move without delay. Not moving means to be a living being, without moving away from being a living being. That's awakening.

This is how bodhisattvas help people. We help ourselves and we help others by witnessing the way all things advance and confirm themselves. This is the practice of suchness, which has been intimately communicated by buddhas and ancestors. Now you have it, so please keep it well.

Green Dragon Temple
Green Gulch Farm
Muir Beach, California
February 1987

FIFTEEN

✹

Listen to the Body

Our most recent *sesshin* was dedicated to the practice and teaching of Dainin Katagiri Roshi. At the end of that *sesshin*, I shared a vision of all of us sitting in a circle. At the center of the circle, I put the name of our great compassionate teacher Dainin, "Great Patience." All of us in the circle had sat through suffering during the *sesshin*, visible suffering and invisible suffering. At that time, I talked about the way each person coped with the suffering: the way she sat and lived with her individual difficulty.

Beginning from where we ended then, we again sit with the realization that as we sit, there is suffering in the center of our circle. That suffering appears in our lives and it appears throughout the world. There are many forest fires burning in California now. Our country seems to be on the brink of another war, and some of us have friends and family members in the armed forces or living in the Middle East. Although you all know it, I want to say again that *sesshin* means sitting here with the truth of suffering. With that truth first we sit. We are fortunate to be able to sit, to find our way of peace and joy, given the suffering we will experience here in this room and all around us. We're fortunate that we have this sitting practice, and that we now have the opportunity to follow it intensively for seven days.

Right now, the sky is overcast. A light mist is in the air, but the sun may come out any minute. Our feelings may change. We may become happier; we may becomes sadder. But there is something that remains unmoved in the midst of the comings and goings of our happiness: something completely still, silent, and at peace right under our nosess.

Begin this *sesshin* by listening to your body. Listen to that which is affected by light and sound, tastes and odors, and tactile things, such as heat, cold, pressure, roughness, and smoothness. Listen to something that is upright, something that responds to these phenomena. This is similar to saying, Please listen to silence. By listening to your body, perhaps you can better understand that silence has structure, that silence is not nothing. There is a function in silence. There is responsiveness in silence. Sitting still and listening to the body may reveal this structure, function, and responsiveness. So while sitting still, please listen to the body. I am suggesting this as a way to realize peace in the midst of suffering. Listen to the body.

At the beginning of another *sesshin*, Katagiri Roshi said, "Don't make zazen into a toy." Don't think that you are sitting here doing something. That is making zazen into a toy: a thing you can manipulate. Rather, try to realize what it means to be completely alone. This aloneness means that there is not something else besides you that is called another person. There is not something else besides you that is called zazen. You are completely alone and that is zazen. Absolute aloneness. This is the same as "Listen to the body." "Listen to the body" is about how to be absolutely alone.

Buddha taught what he called "the better way to live alone" in the Theranamo Sutra. Here is a new translation of it by Thich Nhat Hanh. It is short; I made a few gender changes. Please listen:

"I heard these words of the Buddha one time when the Lord was staying at the monastery in the Jeta Grove, in the town of Sravasti. At that time there was a monk named Thera (Elder), who always preferred to be alone. Whenever he could, he praised the practice of living alone. He sought alms alone and sat in meditation alone.

"One time a group of *bhikkhus* came to the Lord, paid their respect by prostrating at his feet, stepped to one side, sat down at a distance, and said, 'Blessed One, there is an elder by the name of Thera who only wants to be alone. He always praises the practice of living alone. He goes into the village alone to seek alms, returns home from the village alone, and sits in meditation alone.'

"The Lord Buddha told one of the *bhikkhus*, 'Please go to the place where the monk Thera lives and tell him I wish to see him.'

"The *bhikkhu* obeyed. When the monk Thera heard the Buddha's wish, he came without delay, prostrated at the feet of the Buddha, stepped to one side, and sat down at a distance. Then the Blessed One asked the monk Thera, 'Is it true that you prefer to be alone, praise the life of solitude, go for alms alone, come back to the village alone, and sit in meditation alone?'

"The monk Thera replied, 'It is true, Blessed One.'

"Buddha asked the monk Thera, 'How do you live alone?'

"The monk Thera replied, 'I live alone; no one else lives with me. I praise the practice of being alone. I go for alms alone, and I come back from the village alone. I sit in meditation alone. That is all.'

"Then the Buddha taught the monk as follows: 'It is obvious that you like the practice of living alone. I do not want to deny that, but I want to tell you that there is a wonderful way to be alone. It is the way of deep observation to see that the past no longer exists and the future has not yet come, and to dwell at ease in the present moment, free from desire. When a person lives in this way, [she] has no hesitation in [her] heart. [She] gives up all anxieties and regrets, lets go of all binding desires, and cuts the fetters which prevent [her] from being free. This is called "the better way to live alone." There is no more wonderful way of being alone than this.'

" Then the Blessed One recited this *gatha:*

In observing life deeply,

it is possible to see clearly all that is.

Not enslaved by anything,

it is possible to put aside all craving.

The result is a life of peace and joy.

This is truly to live alone.

"Hearing the Lord's words, the monk Thera was delighted. He prostrated respectfully to the Buddha and departed."[1]

Our Zen practice emphasizes living completely in the present, moment by moment. Here in an early Pali sutra, we see instructions about how to cut away all considerations and bring ourselves to the real present experience. This is what Buddha calls the better way to live alone, which, of course, can be done with others around you; and this is what I am rephrasing as "listen to the body." Listen to the body as a way to drop away the past, drop away the future, and even drop away the present.

I would also like to take this opportunity to mention again the wonderful practice of touching your hands to each other in this mudra we call the concentration, or cosmic, mudra. Please keep this mudra in contact with your abdomen while sitting. Actually touch the hands to the abdomen, and keep actual tactile contact there. Wake up all these sensitive skin surfaces, and touch the abdomen with these hands. Particularly, be aware of the outside of the little fingers touching the cloth covering your abdomen. This helps you enter into awareness of the body. Also, it's an advance guard against drowsiness, because the first thing to go, maybe even before your eyes shut, will be these little fingers. When they slip away from your body, you've got a warning that your attention is drifting. So it's a nice little button to just keep pressing right there. To keep it up is helpful and, I find, very difficult, so don't be hard on yourself if you aren't able to do it right away. You probably will be able to later if you continue to make the effort. It's hard for me, too, but during *sesshin*, as the awareness of suffering increases, this direct physical awareness is a great refuge. So I really recommend that you try to practice this. Convert yourself to bodily awareness.

So start out very simply. To be alone, absolutely alone, to be still and silent and listen to the body is a road to peace and harmony, not only for yourself but for all suffering beings in this world.

Green Dragon Temple
Green Gulch Farm
Muir Beach, California
August 10, 1990

SIXTEEN

✵

The Path of Peace Has No Sign

Sometimes people ask me why in Zen meditation we keep our eyes open. In some forms of meditation, the eyes are shut, and a lot of people find it easier to become calm that way. That's fine. But in Zen practice, we recommend that you meditate with your eyes open. If you look at a buddha statue, I think you'll find that it will probably have its eyes open. Even when buddha is reclining, his eyes are open. Buddhas have their eyes open because they're observing living beings. They're observing living beings with eyes of compassion and eyes of wisdom. They never close their eyes of wisdom. They never close their eyes of compassion. They're always watching living beings.

When we make a buddha statue and put it on an altar, we do what's called an eye-opening ceremony. We recite a verse from the Lotus Sutra describing Avalokiteshvara, the Bodhisattva of Infinite Compassion. "Eyes of compassion observing sentient beings assemble an ocean of blessing, peace, and happiness beyond measure." We say this verse seven times, each time a little bit more enthusiastically. This helps open the eyes of the statue. Our vow as disciples of Buddha is to help all beings become free: to find peace and blessing and happiness. This includes a vow to enter all realms of misery with our eyes open and to observe. Our willingness to join hands with beings in the realms of misery and to walk with them through birth and death in itself assembles peace.

It's not so easy to join hands with all suffering beings and walk with them forever. In order to be successful at this vow, you must practice meditation. With such a great intention, you must harmonize your body and your mind, you must harmonize heaven and Earth. You don't meditate just in order to calm your own mind, although that's part of it. You meditate to become free of the draining sense that you are separate from others. You sit still in the middle of all living beings; you sit with all the buddhas. You develop a soft, pliable body and mind. You develop the willingness to drop off body and mind, to let go of the separation between yourself and all other living beings. You drop the mind that criticizes others. You can't join hands with all beings if you hold to the mind that criticizes. You can't even do it if you hold to the mind that praises. You have to let go of everything.

This doesn't mean that you will lose your critical capacity. You will still be able to see faults in others. It does not mean that you will lose your ability to praise. If you drop the mind that criticizes, that thinks in terms of self and other, that thinks in terms of right and wrong, your whole life will become nothing but praise. But that doesn't mean that you will lose your ability to see problems, like anybody else can.

I heard Gregory Bateson tell a story about Samuel Johnson, the great English writer. One night when he was fairly old, he was doing his midnight meditations, as was his habit, and something terrible started to happen to his body and mind, something very painful and disorienting. He thought his brain was being attacked. He probably was having a stroke. So he immediately kneeled by his bed and prayed to God, saying, "Do whatever you want to my body, but please don't destroy my mind." Being an educated man of the times, he prayed to God in Latin verse. Then he lay down in bed to rest, and he realized that his verses hadn't been very well composed. So he got out of bed and kneeled again and said, in Latin, "Dear gracious and bountiful Lord, thank you very much for preserving my critical capacities." And he went back to bed.

It's not that you lose your abilities, it's that you let go of them. Anything you hold on to causes disharmony.

In my little discussion group yesterday evening, one person talked about how she wanted to be helpful in this world, and yet she just had bought a car. She thought, Now I'm going to drive this car, and I'm totally part of the whole process that is causing so much suffering. While she was talking, I thought, Maybe I should sell my car, and ride a bicycle to San Francisco. But then somebody else would drive my car, and I'll still have to go over the Golden Gate Bridge, I would still be in the pollution. And I would still have to go to the store eventually and buy a new tire. In other words, no matter what you do, you're part of it. But there's some part of you that thinks, Gee, I don't want to be part of it. I want to be pure. I don't want to be part of this huge, destructive machine.

There are two tendencies of our minds: we want to do something, and we want to be free of doing something. There's a Zen story about this. A teacher named Wind Cave (Fengxue), said to his monks, "If you raise a speck of dust the nation flourishes, but the elders furrow their brows. If you don't raise a speck of dust, the nation perishes, but the elders relax their brows."[1] Raising a speck of dust means many things. One meaning is more or less literal: building a house, establishing a Zen center, starting a Buddhist Peace Fellowship, organizing a Nevada Desert Experience.[2] If you set up something like that, the nation flourishes. You have a nice temple, you have a nice organization. But the elders look at that and say, "What are those people doing? What are they doing setting up a Zen center?" The nation flourishes, but you also get what's called skillful generals and crafty ministers. And people build test sites for big bombs to protect the people in the flourishing country. Other people want to be pure and free from craftiness and defensiveness. They say, "I'm not part of that." In ancient China, people who wanted to avoid the defiled world of politics were willing to go off to the mountains and eat mushrooms and roots and even die of starvation out of their desire to be pure.

Both those tendencies are errors. Anything we do is an error. If you do something, then you suffer; if you don't do something, then you suffer: either way, you get in trouble. There's a way that's not doing either one of those things, which is just to be with people, yourself included. Be with the sufferings caused by human action. That path is the path of blessing.

How do we harmonize these tendencies? We can admit—constantly admit—our errors. Constantly admit, "I want to be part of this. Hey, I don't want to be part of this." We can watch our minds veer off toward these two extremes. And we can balance meditation and action. And harmonize wisdom and compassion.

Much of what goes on at a nuclear test site is "boy play," a symbolic acting out of a certain kind of male energy or male imagery. It may be necessary for men, or even women, to imagine this process of digging into the ground and going boom! We should understand that this imaginative process may be useful. It may be what they have to do as part of their individual development, because there's something in their psyches that has to be dealt with, but it doesn't need to be acted out. That causes problems. It can be dealt with at the level of imagination. If that opportunity is not offered, then some people will be driven, consciously or unconsciously, to a more gross or concrete expression of violence.

In order to divert energy away from acting out these destructive tendencies, we must be sympathetic to them, because otherwise we won't understand how to direct the energy in a wholesome way. If we just think they are bad and try to eliminate them, it won't work. If we can sympathize with these tendencies and realize that they're in us, too, then we can help.

Another thing we need to learn is that we're just fine. We're complete right now and, at the same time, we can evolve, we can transcend ourselves. Our completeness includes the possibility of improvement.

We need to realize that nothing matters. The desert doesn't matter, Las Vegas doesn't matter, I don't matter, and you don't matter. We need to realize this. Realizing this is the basis for realizing that everything matters. If we don't understand that nothing matters, then we're going to think that just some things matter. We're going to think that some things are more important than other things. And the things that we think matter will vary from person to person. Some of us will think, We matter but the people at the test site don't. Or they'll think that the people at the test site matter but we don't. But if you realize with your wisdom eye that nothing matters, then you can realize that everything matters, that every inch of ground on this planet is sacred. We say in Soto Zen, "There's no place in the whole world where you can spit." Everything matters, everything is important.

One of my favorite stories in Zen literature is where one of our ancestors—it was Seigen Gyoshi—was asked, "What is the essential meaning of the Buddha's teaching?"

And he replied, "What is the price of rice in Luling?"[3]

I translate that to modern terms as, "What is the price of gas in Las Vegas?" You might say, That's different, because rice is necessary and gas isn't. But these days, people think that gas is necessary. So from a Buddhist perspective, we can ask what it costs for this gas to be here, the gas we are putting in our cars here in Las Vegas. What does it take to get that gas there? How many nuclear tests? How many wars? What does it take for us to get that gas at that price? Meditate on that. Look at Las Vegas, look at Los Angeles, look at San Francisco, and try to figure it out: How much does it cost for you to have that gas? For anybody to have that gas? Study that. Observe that. That's the meaning of Buddhism. There's no end to the cost of that gas. There's no end to the cost of our rice and our clothing. That's the meaning of our practice. Sit in the middle of Las Vegas, and study the cost of gas.

We're coming here to witness one of the most horrible costs of gas. We're quietly, alertly observing our pain as we observe the cost of the gas. We're supporting one another in this meditation, because it's hard for one of us to go out to the test site alone and observe it.

Somebody asked me how she could just sit when she saw the oceans dying and the fish dying and she felt so passionate about taking action for the environment. It's fine to be passionate about these matters. I'm suggesting that you sit in the middle of your passion. If you do, your passion will not be limited. If you just run to take care of what you already see, without first settling down in the middle of your passion, then you'll still have a limited view of what you need to do. You'll become self-righteous, because you'll say, "I'm doing what's most important here. How can those other people be concerned with those other minor things?" But no matter what we do, we are also overlooking many other things that need attention. If you realize the vastness of your responsibility, you don't think that the tiny bit you do is the whole thing. In the great ocean of beneficial action, we all have to specialize, but we can remember that our work is just a circle of water, not the whole ocean. As human beings, we always have a limited view, and we should acknowledge that. So in order to really be helpful, I'm afraid we must sit.

Just sitting is something you can do while you're walking around on the nuclear test site. Just sitting is something you can do while you're in the slums, while you're riding in a car, or while you're meditating on the cost of gas. Just sitting means you're at the center of all suffering, and you're not being biased in your positioning of yourself in this world. That's what just sitting means. And it's not easy. What's easy is to go off to some extreme.

The story about Seigen and the price of rice is celebrated by a poem, which goes like this:

The accomplishing work of great peace has
no sign;
The family way of peasants is most pristine—
Only concerned with village songs and festival
drinking,
How would they know of the virtues of Shun
or the benevolence of Yao?[4]

We must remember that the path of peace has no sign. We can't say beforehand what peace will look like, or what we need to do to bring it about. Peace is not some fixed thing. Peace is welcoming us but we must find it. We have to bring it alive. Right now. We don't know what it is beforehand. We must give up our preconceptions about what brings peace: otherwise, it's an error.

This weekend together is our village songs and festival drinking. Our being together, our sitting together, our discussions, our eating and drinking together, and our going out in the desert together and witnessing the damage: this is what the ancestor meant by "only concerned with village songs and festival drinking." When we go back to San Francisco and other places, when we return to our home villages, we can continue to observe all living beings with eyes of compassion. This observation, although it may be painful, should be festive, too—it should be joyful.

Because this path of peace has no sign, we don't have to have any special equipment. Because it has no sign, it can be accomplished in any situation, moment by moment. It needs only the circumstances that meet us in each situation, and it can use only those circumstances. We have to find our way with all the people, all the living beings who are there with us at that moment. We have to discover how to sing our village song.

When we're discussing very serious topics such as nuclear disarmament, I often remember what Suzuki Roshi said: "What we're doing is far too important to be taken seriously." So maybe it would be good to end by singing a happy song. This is one of my favorite Zen songs. I think it's about how to walk the signless path of peace. Would you please sing it with me? It's called "When The Red, Red, Robin Comes Bob, Bob, Bobbin' Along." Do you know that song?

When The Red, Red, Robin
Comes Bob, Bob, Bobbin' Along

When The Red, Red, Robin
Comes Bob, Bob, Bobbin'
Along, along,
There'll be no more sobbin'
When he starts throbbin'
his old sweet song,
Wake up, wake up you sleepy head,
Get up, get up, get out of bed,
Cheer up, cheer up, the sun is red,
Live, Love, laugh, and be happy,
What if I've been blue
now I'm walkin' through
fields of flow'rs,
Rain may glisten
but still I listen
for hours and hours.
I'm just a kid again
doin' what I did again
singing a song
When The Red, Red, Robin
Comes Bob, Bob, Bobbin' Along.[5]

Nevada Nuclear Test Site
Las Vegas, Nevada
April 1994

SEVENTEEN

❂

Father's Day

I've been thinking about Father's Day and what it means to be a father, and I remembered that the Hebrew way of saying father is *abba*, which is the root of *abbot*. I realized that an abbot and a father are quite similar. By coincidence, in this life, I have received the title of both father and abbot, so I can speak about these two roles from my own experience. I might be expected to speak loudly about them, but I want to whisper, so that there's a contradiction in my speech.

My talk, then, is about fatherhood, abbothood, and Buddha's way. Buddha's way can be described in infinite ways, but one way to describe it is as the study of the self. To study the self means to study the relationship between self and other. It means to be honest about what I am, so honest that I realize clearly what I'm not; and what I'm not is called the other. Studying this relationship between self and other is difficult, because there's a contradiction: "self and other" is not really something that can be established, and yet much of the time I live according to that separation.

So when it comes to being a father and an abbot and to studying the way, they're all difficult for me. They all involve painful contradictions between my responsibility, my authority, and others. Studying this relationship is something I have not done very well. I have not been a very good father or abbot or student of the way. This is simply honest. To convey my feelings about this, I want to recite a poem by Peter Meinke called "This is a poem to my son Peter."

this is a poem to my son Peter

whom I have hurt a thousand times

whose large and vulnerable eyes

have glazed in pain at my ragings

thin wrists and fingers hung

boneless in despair, pale freckled back

bent in defeat, pillow soaked

by my failure to understand.

I have scarred through weakness

and impatience your frail confidence forever

because when I needed to strike

you were there to be hurt and because

I thought you knew

you were beautiful and fair

your bright eyes and hair

but now I see that no one knows that

about himself, but must be told

and retold until it takes hold

because I think anything can be killed

after a while, especially beauty

so I write this for life, for love, for

you, my oldest son Peter, age 10,

going on 11.[1]

This resonates with the way I've been a father,

with the way I've been an abbot, with the way I take care of myself, and also with the way I've been taken care of. I don't know if my tears are for my sons and daughters and for the students who have trusted me, or if they are for myself.

The most important thing for an abbot is to know the hearts of the community. I propose that to know the hearts of others, you must know your own heart. If you skip over your own heart and don't take care of it or study it, how will you be able to see where others' hearts start?

If we study our relationships with others and if we study ourselves, we will see what our work is. What we often do, especially we men who have the title of father or abbot, is think we have some job to do, and we work on fulfilling that job, believing that we don't have time to look at ourselves. But our real work comes forth from studying the self and studying the relationship between self and others and between self and the environment.

I must admit that in trying to fulfill my responsibility as abbot, I did not pay enough attention to my daughter or to the little girl who lives inside of me. I didn't think that was my job. Now I see that it is my job and that if I take care of the little girl inside of me, I will take better care of my job as abbot. But it took me a long time and a lot of suffering to see that. Often in the past, when this little girl inside me was hurt, I would say, "Don't worry, dear, I'll get rid of your enemies," rather than ask, "How are you feeling? What do you want to do now?" She didn't want defense: she wanted attention. She didn't want me to eliminate those who had hurt her feelings: she wanted me to take her home. But I was more into protecting than listening, more into defending than directly addressing her pain. In this way, I was not a very good father to my own heart, and so, of course, I did the same thing with the big girls who were practicing with me.

In thinking about all of this, I remembered a dream that I had recently. In the dream, as in real life, I was a person who had a lot of appointments. Because of the growth of Zen Center, I am in a position today where a lot of people want to talk to me. In the dream, I was going to an appointment I had with somebody, and I realized that I was late for another appointment with somebody else. Then my secretary told me, "You have to catch a three o'clock plane, and it's almost three o'clock now," and someone else came up to me and said, "I need to talk to you." This went on for quite a while, and in the dream I wasn't worried, because this is my normal life.

In the middle of all this, someone else came to me and asked me to join a search party for a little boy who was lost. I thought, Okay, I'll be part of this search. Even though I'd never seen this boy, I knew what he looked like. He was about five years old, with blond hair and a light complexion. When I saw him in my mind's eye, I realized that he was either autistic or had Down's syndrome: he wasn't capable of what we consider normal social interactions.

Even though I'd agreed to be on the search party, I balked when the woman in charge said that we would be getting briefed about how to search. I thought, Wait a minute! I'm willing to go look for this kid, but I'm not going to go to school to learn *how* to look for him. That's too much. I mean, this is a sideline as it is. I'm a busy man.

Afterward I thought, In Zen practice, you should take everything on with the intention of doing it thoroughly. I saw that I was willing to be thorough about trying to take care of the many contradictory responsibilities that I had with all these different people wanting various things, but that I wasn't willing to give my complete devotion to looking for this kid or being instructed about how to look for him. I felt ashamed of that.

The other day, someone showed me a passage from a book that said that until we get a kind of unhappy sense that nothing matters, we will not realize that everything matters. Somehow, going down into the pit where we don't care about anything, where nothing matters, is necessary before we care about everything.

Reflecting on my dream, I realized that my real work is to look for that disabled boy, that boy who can't do anything, who can't tell the difference between himself and other people. One of our scriptures says, "Like a babe in the world, in five aspects complete, who can't rise or stand or walk or talk." This is a description of a buddha. There's somebody inside who is totally disabled, who can't do anything himself, who is enabled only by others.

Another way to see this is to watch how "Nothing matters" turns into "Everything matters": how lack of meaning turns into meaning. There's a very close relationship between meaninglessness and meaning. I propose that each of us walks around with some sense of meaning, but maybe it's not very deep, and the way to deepen that meaning is to open up to the terrors of eternity: the beautiful terrors of eternity, where certain things don't make sense anymore. Consulting this beautiful terror, we may come back with a deeper meaning. But often we don't want to look at it. It may be too scary.

Earlier I said that I had been given the title of father and the title of abbot. Both of those were given to me. I never told my daughter to call me Daddy, but somehow she came up with that name for me, in a house where it would have been all right if she had called me Reb. She gave me the title of daddy. I don't feel worthy of that gift, but she gave it to me anyway. And a community of people gave me the title of abbot: this is a gift to me. These people let me play these roles of father and abbot. These titles aren't possible without somebody giving them to you.

There's also some giving involved in making a baby in the first place. You can't have a father without a mother. These days, some people think you can have a mother without a father. I don't dare comment on that scenario: I'm not up to date on that. But I say you can't have a father without a mother, and you can't have a mother without a child, and you can't have a child without a mother, and you can't have a child without a father, and you can't have a father without a child. It isn't only that you can't have a father without a child: you can't have a child without a father. All these things make each other. This is Buddha's main teaching. It's called dependent co-arising: that everything comes forth from all directions in the universe to make each thing, and that this coming forth is what gives each thing authority.

Everything has authority because everything is the arrival of everything else. Everything is a realization of the rest of the world. That makes each thing important, and that makes everything matter. But somehow, unless you first sense that nothing matters, unless you give up everything, you don't see that everything deserves your complete attention because everything has radiant authority. Everything. This is Zen. We say there's no place in the world you can spit. In other words, there's no place that's unimportant, that's a low-quality place, of which you could say, "Well, I can spit there." There's no place on Earth like that, so if you do spit, you should realize that you are spitting in a precious place and maybe you should brush your teeth first before you spit.

In my dream, the stupid boy doesn't know, "This is a good place" and "That is a bad place." He respects every place because every place is his life. He has no place where he says, "Oh, this isn't my life." He's too dumb to figure that out. He just thinks, life-life-life-life. Not "Oh, this thing here is my big responsibility as abbot, and this over here is a measly family responsibility. This is my responsibility for all sentient beings, to the big community, and to the cultural evolution of Zen in America, and this other thing is unimportant." He's too dumb.

When my daughter was about three, I took her to see a Walt Disney movie called *Song of the South.* In one scene, the little girl put on a party dress and started walking to a party. On the way, some big boys teased her and pushed her down into a mud puddle, and she got her party dress all muddy. They said something like, "Oh, we can clean it," but she didn't want to go to the party anymore. She didn't want to just snap out of it, like everything was okay. She didn't want to sing and dance. She was too hurt. She just wanted to cry, and she did, very nicely. My little daughter, sitting next to me, burst into tears, too. I told her it was just a movie, but she was inconsolable. She was not going to stop crying, she'd had enough of the movie, and she wanted to go home. And so we left. But I didn't really understand her motivation. I thought it would be okay for her to watch somebody cry, to cry a little bit, and then to continue watching the movie. But that wasn't the way it was for her.

This past winter in the mountains, I heard and understood that little girl who doesn't want to play anymore because her party dress got mud on it. That's just the way it is sometimes. I dedicated myself to giving that little girl more attention, to not protecting her from that kind of experience but to listening to her. So in that way, my daughter taught me about myself.

When my daughter was little, one of my jobs at home was to bathe her. Then when she was eight, I told her that I thought she was getting too big for us to take baths together anymore. I was pretty much the same size as I had been throughout her lifetime, but she was getting bigger and bigger and getting to be more like her mother physically, closer in size and shape and way of moving. She didn't like the idea of our not taking baths together anymore and asked why we had to stop. I said, "Have you noticed that you're more like your mom than you are like me? Wouldn't you think it was funny if your mom took a bath with your grandfather? Wouldn't that seem funny?" She agreed that it would. I said, "And that's the reason, it's just kind of funny. Every day you're getting to be more like your mother, and you and me taking a bath together is getting to be more like your mom and your grandfather taking a bath together."

She could see that. A few minutes later, she came into our bedroom and stuck her head in the door, which was not her usual way. Usually, she would just barge in as though she owned the place and say, "Me be mibble," which meant "Me be in the middle," as in "Okay, you two separate, and let me be in the middle." But this time, she acted as though our room was not her room. By sticking her head in first, she was recognizing a degree of separation between us. Because that's what was starting to happen: I was separating from her. I was separating from someone who from the time she was born was as close to me as anyone could be, someone who could vomit in my face with total impunity. Because what was inside her was the same as what was inside me, no difference. But now I had to separate from her. It seemed appropriate. It's part of growing up.

Now, approximately a decade later, I can hardly believe that I used to take baths with her. It seems strange that

I was so close to her in that way. Now my relationship with her is more spiritual, and we're in the process of discovering how we are still connected and how we can reconnect.

There is in your heart and in everything about you an authority, an authority given to you by all things. And for the purposes of your development, you have a father to look at and to give authority to so you can eventually see it in yourself. You loan it to him. In spiritual matters, you can loan this same authority, this inner authority of our heart, to a woman, too. In that sense, you can have a "female father," a woman who becomes an external reflection with whom you work to help you find your own inner authority. Loaning someone your authority is difficult, of course, because of the danger of completely giving away your own authority. But somehow you need to project it outside of yourself because you have trouble seeing it inside. "I thought you knew / you were beautiful and fair / your bright eyes and hair / but now I see that no one knows that / about himself, but must be told . . . "[2]

And who is going to tell you? Of course, a mother can tell you, and she often does, by saying, "You're just like me. I care about you just like I care about myself—even more." She just looks at you and you see that.

But I propose that the father must tell you, too. He's not you: he's external. You didn't come from his body. He's the guy who goes out during the day and comes back at night or comes to visit from out of town and maybe plays with you. And you give him authority. You respect him, so when he tells us you that you're beautiful and important, it works. I don't feel that the problem lies in holding back from giving or loaning the father authority. People do that with incredible generosity. I think that little girls and little boys, when they see that guy who is not around very much, pull out the authority and throw it at him and say, "Here, take it. You can be my dad. Yeah, I'd like you around more, but I'll give it to you anyway, because I need to see it and hear it back from you."

My own father left me when I was eleven. Before that, he told me many times that I was beautiful. Many times. He told me that I was strong, he told me that he wanted me to be able to hit that ball, tote that barge, lift that bale. He told me that he loved me and that I had to do it myself. That was helpful to me, but then he left. So I went out and I gave that same authority to my algebra teacher, my football coach, my track coach. They received my gift and gave it back to me and said, "You're beautiful, you're great." They told me over and over again until it took hold. One time is not enough, because you don't know that about yourself. Telling yourself is both possible and helpful, but it's not sufficient. The other thing—of being told and retold by an external authority—is also necessary.

When you are given that role, that responsibility by another, you have to do your job. You have to put that girl and boy in your heart and walk around with them and adore them and say you see them. You have to do that. And I have not done a very good job of it. But I say all this ". . . for life, for love, for / you, my oldest son Peter, age 10, / going on 11."[3] Happy Father's Day. Please call your father and tell him something, even if he's dead. I call my father right now and say, "Thank you."

Green Dragon Temple
Green Gulch Farm
Muir Beach, California
June 20, 1993

EIGHTEEN

✸

The End of Suffering:
A Christmas Koan

Nagarjuna once said,
Without a foundation in the
conventional truth,
The significance of the ultimate
cannot be taught.
Without understanding the
significance of the ultimate,
Liberation is not achieved.[1]

Without relying on everyday common practices, the ultimate truth cannot be expressed. Without approaching the ultimate truth, nirvana cannot be attained. Zen stories often indicate the ultimate truth.

A monk asked Zhaozhou, "In the eon of emptiness, is there still someone cultivating practice?"

Zhaozhou said, "What do you mean by the eon of emptiness?"

The monk said, "That is when not a single thing exists."

Zhaozhou said, "Only this can be called ultimate practice."

If I say, This is where not a single thing exists, it sounds as though I'm bringing up the ultimate truth. When I bring that up, I hope that you have suffered enough in this lifetime to realize that I dare teach this ultimate truth only after you have studied and been relying on the relative truth for a long time. The relative truth is that suffering appears in this world, that you and I are separate, and that this clinging to separate existence is the origin of suffering. This is relative truth. The ultimate truth is that there is nobody separate from anybody, that there is not one single thing that exists by itself. I hope that when I say that, you don't think it means that there is nothing there. Please understand that "not a single thing exists" means that there is not a single thing existing by itself, that there is no person existing by herself.

The monk said, "That is when not a single thing exists," and Zhaozhou said, "Only this can be called ultimate practice." The eon of emptiness is a time and a place where things do not exist on their own. Can you imagine a world where nothing appears by itself, where each thing comes up with everything, where everything comes up by the kindness of everything? Everything comes up with the support of everything, and everything that comes up supports everything. Only this can be called ultimate practice. But we rely on the relative truth in order to receive this ultimate teaching. We rely on the relative truth that "I by myself practice Zen." This is practicing relative truth. I myself suffer, you yourself suffer. We rely on this as our base, and it is there that we receive the teaching that everything is liberated right now and nothing is tied down.

In the realm where not a single thing exists by

itself, anything is possible. In the eon of emptiness anything can happen. When things exist by themselves, the possibilities are radically constricted. Only women bear children. It may not seem to be a problem that only women can bear children. But if we think so, then we have not studied relative truth completely. It's painful for us when we can't give birth. That is one reason why men go to war. Although war is horrible and destructive, still, it gives some men access to the radiance and vitality of creation. This is the realm of relative truth.

In the Prajna Paramita Sutra, Subhuti asked Buddha from where does a bodhisattva go forth into the practice of wisdom beyond wisdom? Buddha said that one goes forth from the relative world. If you don't put your foot down fully on the earth, you cannot go forward; if you go forward without really accepting the relative truth, you will misunderstand the ultimate.

In the world of relative truth, you think that you can't be yourself. You might think, I can be creative and think of something almost impossible, but will they let me do it? If I were just myself, I would take my clothes off at the airport. But they might punish me, so I can't be myself. This is the relative world. You can be yourself a little, but not completely.

In the relative world, if somebody says that she has trouble staying awake in zazen and asks me how to stay awake, I may say, Try getting more sleep, or run around the block before you sit, or have some green tea, or open your eyes wider. Look at the spot between your eyebrows;

look higher on the wall; chant the Heart Sutra; chant the bodhisattva vows to yourself; consider how little time you have left, and so on. When the grass around my house gets yellow, I go to the garden and get compost to put on it. The little grasses stand up and turn green: they like it. But if there is no compost or if I am too busy, then they stay yellow. Still, I do my best to stay awake, and to help others stay awake, to help the grasses grow. This is the relative world, and it's not workable, really. You may think it is not so bad. But really, it's not going to work out. Pretty soon you are going to see that, if you don't already see it. If you do see it, you may have studied the relative world long enough and be ready to practice the ultimate without becoming misled.

If you study the world of suffering, then you will become aware of your lack of faith and practice. You will become aware that you do not really trust this world. If you think that you really trust the world, do you really trust suffering? Don't you have a little problem with it? Don't you have a little doubt? Don't you think a little bit that there is something that you can't do? Don't you feel a little limited, a little trapped? Where's the world where you can actually just express yourself spontaneously? Where's the world where you are not an independent agent who is trapped and tied up?

If you have not studied the world where you are trapped thoroughly enough to realize that you are trapped, and you think that you are free, actually you are still in the world where you are trapped. You are just dreaming that you are free and that you can do whatever you want. But you can't. Everything you do in the world as an independent agent is going to cause problems for yourself and others. If you do not understand this point, then you haven't studied long enough to enter the ultimate practice from which you can act spontaneously. When you are no longer acting as an independent agent, everything that you do will be harmless and you will see that everybody is supporting you. Everybody does support you in the world where not a single thing exists. You have to experience the world where you are tight, limited, and anxious. It's there that you turn and wake up to the world where you spontaneously do the right thing. In the world where there is not a single thing, you can just be yourself. You can just be yourself when yourself is not a single thing.

The practice of sitting is a ritual expression of the teaching that you can just be yourself. Just sitting means you can realize the way in any posture. It means you can lie down. It means you don't have to force yourself to sit still. Manjushri gave Buddha a little talk one time and basically what he said was that when a person is just a person, this is what we mean by being awake. After his talk, a bunch of upstanding citizens of Buddha's world came up to Manjushri and said, "You are really incredibly wise, just like your name says; you are like sweetness and light throughout the universe. You are fantastic, the foremost sage."

He said, "Oh yeah? Well, actually, you should call me the utmost exponent of greed, hate, and delusion. You should call me the utmost enslaved suffering being. You should call me the utmost bum. I'm an ordinary person, I'm the foremost of the ordinary."

Most people in society cannot stand to be just ordinary. So we have Zen centers to train people to be patient and accept their ordinariness. Manjushri went all the way to become a completely ordinary person. Thus he realized that there is really no such thing as an ordinary person living all by herself. This is called waking up. When someone is having trouble staying awake, I can give her some advice. But actually, the ultimate practice is, if you are having trouble staying awake, have trouble staying awake. It's okay to try to stay awake when you are having trouble staying awake. It's all right to be a person trying to stay awake. But before you do anything, first of all, be this person and feel what it is like to be a person who is stuck in this state. Being this person is your ticket, your price of admission, into the eon of emptiness. Being this person is the way to practice just sitting.

You don't get to be this person by your own personal power. As soon as you are completely this person, you immediately leap beyond the bounds of this person. One of the things that this person can do is to doubt and resist being this person. A person is capable of doing this. When you are in some state, if it is not really great, you imagine some way to make it better. If it is great, you think of ways to protect it; and that's fine. That is the relative world. But you should know that at exactly the same time, there is always one who is not concerned with protecting or avoiding any state. This unconcerned one realizes that everybody is helping him, realizes that everybody is helping him to be irritable or happy or whatever.

We cannot be irritable all by ourselves. Everybody has to help us. We can't go to sleep by ourselves; we can't have a hard time; we can't do anything all by ourselves. We can't even feel unloved by ourselves. We can't feel not appreciated by ourselves. We can't experience injustice by ourselves. We also can't experience justice and love by ourselves. Everybody helps us with everything. So the world where we are miserable and irritable and unrecognized and unloved is ultimately the world where not a single thing exists, because we do not exist singly. Right in our misery, we are completely supported and completely loved and completely free to suffer. If we weren't free to suffer, then we wouldn't be able to. We cannot suffer unless we are allowed to suffer.

When we are joyfully strolling through the Green Gulch gardens on a sunny day, we might think that we are being allowed to stroll through the gardens, and supported so we can stroll through the gardens, and we might say, Thank you. But when we are suffering, do we see that we are being allowed to suffer, that we are being lovingly supported so that we can suffer? Very few people understand that. Even if we do think that way, we probably take it to mean that others are causing us to suffer. Then we blame others rather than thanking them for their kind support.

In the world where I think that I can do things by myself, I don't say thank you to the people who are around me for supporting me and aiding me in my suffering. I feel bad about my suffering, I feel trapped by my suffering, and I feel entangled in my suffering, because I think that I can do something by myself. But when I no longer fall for that and I'm just suffering, then I realize that everybody is helping me, because I couldn't do this suffering by myself. When you realize that everybody is helping you suffer, that is the end of suffering. The expression of suffering doesn't necessarily go away, but you are liberated: you get the joke. In the realm of not a single thing exists, when you are suffering, you say thank you. You feel grateful. When you are suffering and you feel grateful, this is called the end of suffering.

All of us in this *sesshin* are intimate with this process. We are all suffering but at a certain point, we start feeling grateful in the middle of the same suffering. What is happening? How does this work? Gradually, by hit and miss, we allow ourselves to be these suffering people. By the act of being these suffering people, just as we are, we enter the realm where not a single thing exists, and here we are always grateful.

In the realm of being just as you are, anything is possible. How do you enter this realm of unlimited possibility? By tuning in completely to your limited position in the relative world. You tune in by your body, speech, and mind. Right then, the fact of the way you are actually makes anything possible. The way you are is a momentary, fleeting production of the entire universe delivered at this time and place. It seems to be something, but it is just a soft, flexible overlay on top of unlimited potential. It's just a fleeting thin film of appearance over infinite radiance. But you must completely tune in to such a phenomenon. You must not look forward to it or shrink back from it. If you don't tune in to it, this thin film becomes an iron door, bound and double-chained. Even if the body happens to be golden and blissful, you still have to tune in to that body. Tuning in means you just tune in to golden bliss and stop, you don't tune in and cuddle it. You just tune in to it being that way, the same as with some crazy, sick, twisted mind or some yucky verbal expression or some painful, sick body. You just tune in to that form. That's it. The practice is not that golden buddha, it's not that green monster, it's not that sick person, it's not that healthy person, it's not that nice verbal expression, and it's not that mean voice: it's not those things. That's not the practice; that's not Buddhism; that's not Zen. Zen is simply that those things are as they are. Zen is the practice of tuning in to the phenomenal present. You need enough faith to tune in exactly, all the way, and not a little less or more.

Whatever we do, there are consequences. If we wear too much makeup, there will be consequences. If we don't wear any, there will be consequences. If we shave our heads, there will be consequences. Considering the worldly consequences of our actions, we may feel hesitant, hindered, and hemmed in. But there is one thing that the world cannot hinder us from, and that is being who we are at this moment. As a matter of fact, this is exactly what the whole world is assisting us in being.

There are many stories about people who do not accept Buddha's compassion and thus do not feel allowed to be or supported in being just who they are. These people are miserly with themselves and with others. Charles Dickens wrote a book about this, *A Christmas Carol*. In this book, on Christmas Eve, the old miser Scrooge is visited by various ghosts. The first ghost is his late partner, Jacob Marley. Marley is very upset: he isn't a happy ghost, but he isn't a mean ghost either. He doesn't come to hurt Scrooge or even to scare Scrooge. He comes to help Scrooge, to tell him how awful it is not to live your life fully every moment. He comes to tell Scrooge how terrible it is not to practice Zen, the path of compassion for ourselves and others.

Marley warns Scrooge that we will be "captive, bound, and double-ironed,"[2] if we do not understand that for eons immortal beings have constantly labored for the welfare of this Earth, and this good may be wasted if we don't do our part of being thoroughly ourselves. He warns further that if we don't understand this, "'no space of regret can make amends for one life's opportunity misused! Yet such was I! Oh! such was I!'

"'But you were always a good man of business, Jacob,' faltered Scrooge, who now began to apply this to himself.

"'Business!' cried the Ghost, wringing his hands again. 'Mankind was my business. The common welfare was my business; charity, mercy, forbearance, and benevolence, were, all, my business. The dealings of my trade were but a drop of water in the comprehensive ocean of my business!'"[3]

Three more terrifying spirits also visit Scrooge that night. Finally, Scrooge is able to accept their compassion, allowing himself to be himself, and thus unleashing his own vast potential for generosity, mercy, forbearance, and benevolence. Zen is simply the key that opens the door to our vast potential for goodness. It is, much of the time, a hard key and a cold key. Opening the door means tuning in to what we are, how we think, what we say, and what we do with our bodies. We must be thorough; we must thoroughly be who we are in each moment throughout the day without expecting anything for it. Opening the door can be a difficult thing. But we must open the door in order to penetrate the thin layer of illusion that is blocking us from our unlimited, spontaneous available goodness.

Green Dragon Temple
Green Gulch Farm
Muir Beach, California
August 13, 1994

APPENDIX

Notes

Part One

"Great Wisdom Beyond Wisdom Heart Sutra," in *Daily Sutra Book* (San Francisco: San Francisco Zen Center, 1998).

Chapter 3

1. Takakusu Junjiro, ed., "Blue Cliff Record," case 22, in *Taisho Shinshu Daizokyo* (Tokyo: Shuppan Kai, 1922–1933), vol. 48, no. 2003.

2. Wang Wei, *Hiding the Universe: poems* (New York: Grossman, 1972), 40. Author's translation.

3. Dongshan Liangjie, "Song of the Jewel Mirror Samadhi," in *Daily Sutra Book* (San Francisco: San Francisco Zen Center, 1998).

Chapter 4

1. Wang Wei, op. cit. Author's translation.

2. Kishizawa Ian, *Lectures on Shobogenzo.* Author's translation.

Chapter 6

1. *Uddana*, 1:10. Author's translation from original Pali.

2. Takakusu Junjiro, ed., "Transmission of Light by Keizan," case 22, in *Taisho Shinshu Daizokyo* (Tokyo: Shuppan Kai, 1922–1933), vol. 82, no. 2585.

3. Ibid., case 23.

4. Ibid., case 30.

5. George Herbert, "Love," in *The Norton Anthology of English Literature*, ed. M. H. Abrams et al. (New York: W. W. Norton, 1962), vol. I, 841.

Part Two

The Sixteen Great Bodhisattva Precepts, translated by the author and Kazuaki Tanahashi.

Chapter 7

1. Gil Fronsdal, unpublished manuscript.

2. Takakusu Junjiro, ed., "Transmission of Light by Keizan," case 35, in *Taisho Shinshu Daizokyo* (Tokyo: Shuppan Kai, 1922–1933), vol. 82, no. 2585.

3. Eihei Dogen, "Mind of the Way," in *Shobogenzo Doshin* (Tokyo: Eiwanami Shoten, 1940–1967), vol. 3, 243–46. Author's paraphrase.

Chapter 8

1. Takakusu Junjiro, ed., "Essence of Zen Precepts," in *Taisho Shinshu Daizokyo* (Tokyo: Shuppan Kai, 1922–1933), vol. 82, no. 2601. Translated by the author and Kazuaki Tanahashi.

2. Ibid.

Chapter 10

1. Takakusu Junjiro, ed., "Record of Dongshan," in *Taisho Shinshu Daizokyo* (Tokyo: Shuppan Kai, 1922–1933), vol. 47, no. 1986.

2. Henry David Thoreau, *Walden* (1854; reprint, New York: NAL Penguin, 1960), 155.

Chapter 11

Eihei Dogen, "Mountains and Rivers Sutra," in *Shobogenzo Sansuikyo,* (Tokyo: Eiwanami Shoten, 1940–1967), vol. 1, 217–29. Author's translation.

1. William Shakespeare, *Hamlet,* in *Shakespeare: Major Plays and Sonnets,* ed. G. B. Harrison (1601–1602; reprint, New York: Harcourt, Brace & Co., 1948), 1.5.164–67, 616.

Chapter 12

1. Takakusu Junjiro, ed., "Transmission of Light by Keizan," case 46, in *Taisho Shinshu Daizokyo* (Tokyo: Shuppan Kai, 1922–1933), vol. 82, no. 2585.

Part Three

Dongshan Liangjie, "Song of the Jewel Mirror Samadhi," *Daily Sutra Book* (San Francisco: San Francisco Zen Center, 1998).

Chapter 13

1. Han-shan, *Cold Mountain: 100 Poems by the T'ang Poet Han-shan*, trans. Burton Watson (New York: Columbia University Press, 1970), 87.

Chapter 14

1. Takakusu Junjiro, ed., "The Jingde Record of the Transmission of the Lamp," in *Taisho Shinshu Daizokyo* (Tokyo: Shuppan Kai, 1922–1933), vol. 51, no. 2076.

2. Takakusu Junjiro, ed., "Blue Cliff Record," case 22, in *Taisho Shinshu Daizokyo* (Tokyo: Shuppan Kai, 1922–1933), vol. 48, no. 2003.

Chapter 15

1. Thich Nhat Hanh, *Our Appointment with Life: The Buddha's Teaching on Living in the Present* (Berkeley, Calif.: Parallax Press, 1990), 3–4.

Chapter 16

1. Takakusu Junjiro, ed., "Book of Serenity," case 34, in *Taisho Shinshu Daizokyo* (Tokyo: Shuppan Kai, 1922–1933), vol. 48, no 2004.

2. This chapter is adapted from a dharma talk given by Reb Anderson in Las Vegas, Nevada, during the weekend that the Buddhist Peace Fellowship, in association with the Nevada Desert Experience, witnessed at the Nevada nuclear test site, in April 1994. The talk was given the day after the Buddhist Peace

Fellowship group went on a Department of Energy bus tour of the test site and the day before the group returned to the test site for various nonviolent activities: a Buddha's birthday ceremony, a witness, and acts of civil disobedience.

3. Takakusu Junjiro, ed., "Book of Serenity," case 5, in *Taisho Shinshu Daizokyo* (Tokyo: Shuppan Kai, 1922–1933), vol. 48, no 2004.

4. Thomas Cleary, trans., *Book of Serenity* (Hudson, N.Y.: Lindisfarne Press; San Francisco: Wheelwright Press, 1990), 21.

5. Harry Woods, "When The Red, Red, Robin Comes Bob, Bob, Bobbin' Along" (New York: Callicoon Music, 1926).

Chapter 17

1. Peter Meinke, "This is a poem to my son Peter," *Liquid Paper: New and Selected Poems* (Pittsburgh, Penn.: University of Pittsburgh Press, 1991), 46.

2. Ibid.

3. Ibid.

Chapter 18

1. Nagarjuna, *The Fundamental Wisdom of the Middle Way: Nagarjuna's Mulamadhyamakakarika*, trans. Jay L. Garfield (New York: Oxford University Press, 1995), case 24, verse 10, 68.

2. Charles Dickens, *A Christmas Carol* (1843; reprint, New York: Viking Penguin, 1984), 28–29.

3. Ibid.

Appreciations

Grateful acknowledgment is made to the following for permission to reprint previously published material:

Columbia University Press: Excerpt from COLD MOUNTAIN: 100 POEMS BY THE T'ANG POET HAN-SHAN, Burton Watson, ed.; © 1970 Columbia University Press. Reprinted by permission of Columbia University Press.

Oxford University Press: Excerpt from THE FUNDAMENTAL WISDOM OF THE MIDDLE WAY: NAGARJUNA'S MULAMADHYAMAKAKARIKA, by Nagarjuna; translation © 1995 by Jay L. Garfield. Reprinted by permission from Oxford University Press, Inc.

Parallax Press: Excerpt from OUR APPOINTMENT WITH LIFE: THE BUDDHA'S TEACHING ON LIVING IN THE PRESENT, by Thich Nhat Hanh, © 1990. Reprinted by permission from Parallax Press, Berkeley, California.

University of Pittsburg Press: "This is a poem to my son Peter," from LIQUID PAPER: NEW AND SELECTED POEMS, by Peter Meinke, © 1991. Reprinted by permission of the University of Pittsburg Press.

Warner Bros. Publications: WHEN THE RED, RED, ROBIN COMES BOB, BOB, BOBBIN ALONG, by Harry Woods. © 1927 (Renewed) Callicoon Music. Rights for the Extended Renewal Term in the United States controlled by Callicoon Music and administered by The Songwriters Guild of America. All Rights Reserved. Used by permission. Warner Bros. Publications U.S. Inc., Miami, FL 33014.

Bourne Co.: WHEN THE RED, RED, ROBIN (Comes Bob, Bob, Bobbin' Along), by Harry Woods. © 1926 by Bourne Co. (Copyright Renewed). Rights for Extended Renewal Term in the United States of America controlled by Callicoon Music. All rights outside the United States of America controlled by Bourne Co. All Rights Reserved. International Copyright Secured. ASCAP. Reprinted by permission of Bourne Co.

In addition, much appreciation goes to the following:

Photographers: Robert Boni (front cover), Dan Howe (pages 1, 3, and 163), Barbara Wenger (pages 57, 59, and 163, and the author photo on the back cover), and Heather Hiett (pages 105, 107, and 163).

San Francisco Zen Center: For providing us access to their archives to select photographs for use on the cover and within the book. We extend special thanks to Rosalie Curtis and Michael Wenger.

About the Author

Reb Anderson moved to San Francisco from Minnesota, in 1967, to study Zen Buddism with Shunryu Suzuki Roshi, who ordained him as a priest in 1970. Since then, he has continued to practice at San Francisco Zen Center, which includes Beginner's Mind Temple at The City Center (San Francisco), Green Dragon Temple at Green Gulch Farm (near Muir Beach, California), and Zen Mind Temple at Tassajara Zen Mountain Center (Carmel Valley, California). Reb Anderson served as abbot from 1986 to 1995 and is now a senior dharma teacher.

He is particularly interested in Buddhist yoga and psychology, and in the relationship of Buddhist wisdom and compassion to the social and ecological crises of our time. Reb Anderson is currently writing a book on the Buddhist precepts that will be published by Rodmell Press.

He lives with his family and friends at Green Gulch Farm, near Muir Beach, in Northern California, where he teaches, lectures, and leads practice periods. Correspondence to the author can be addressed to Reb Anderson, Green Gulch Farm, 1601 Shoreline Hwy., Sausalito, CA 94965.

About the Editor

Susan Moon is a writer and editor. She is a long-time Zen practitioner and, in recent years, a student of Reb Anderson. She is the author of *The Life and Letters of Tofu Roshi* (a book of humorous fiction) and coeditor (with Lenore Friedman) of *Being Bodies: Buddhist Women on the Paradox of Embodiment,* both from Shambhala Publications. Susan Moon is also the editor of *Turning Wheel: Journal of the Buddhist Peace Fellowship.*

From the Publisher

Rodmell Press publishes books and tapes on yoga and Buddhism. In the *Bhagavadgita* it is written, "Yoga is skill in action." It is our hope that these products will help individuals develop a more skillful practice—one that brings peace to their daily lives and to the Earth.

We thank all whose support, encouragement, and practical advice sustain us in our efforts. In particular, we are grateful to Reb Anderson, B. K. S. Iyengar, and Yvonne Rand for their inspiration.

Our titles are available to the trade from SCB Distributors, 15608 S. New Century Dr., Gardena, CA 90248–2129; 310/532–9400, 800/729–6423, 310/532-7001 (fax), SCB@worldnet.att.net.

For a free copy of our catalog and to receive information on future titles, contact us at

Rodmell Press
2147 Blake St.
Berkeley, CA 94704–2715
510/841–3123
800/841–3123 (order)
510/841–3191 (fax)
RodmellPrs@aol.com